Grace and Freedom in a Secular Age

Grace and Freedom
in a Secular Age

Contingency, Vulnerability, and Hospitality

Philip J. Rossi, SJ

The Catholic University of America Press

Washington, D.C.

Cataloging-in-Publication Data available from the Library of Congress

ISBN: 9780813236261
eISBN: 9780813236278

Contents

Part I
Contingency and the Dynamics of Immanence

Chapter 1

Chapter 2

Part II
Contingency and the Persistence of Grace

Chapter 3

Chapter 4

Chapter 5

Part III
Shaping a World of Grace

Chapter 6

Preface

THIS SHORT VOLUME OFFERS AN overview of the theological import of the philosophical anthropology that Charles Taylor has been patiently articulating in his writings for many decades, most notably in the landmark volumes, *Sources of the Self: The Making of the Modern Identity* and *A Secular Age*. I have constructed this overview by considering key elements of the anthropology he presents in these two sweeping works, while giving an occasional nod to related elements in some of his other writings. Within this overview, Taylor's philosophical anthropology will be understood as his conceptually rich, historically robust, and patiently argued responses to the related questions "What is the human?" and "What significance—if any—does the human have?" I thus will propose that the philosophically articulated responses that Taylor gives to these questions also carry with them a conceptually significant theological subtext that enlarges the scope of these two questions and of the philosophical and theological import of the responses to them that Taylor's work offers. In other words, Taylor's extended effort to frame a philosophical anthropology is articulated in ways that are open to (and indeed invite) orientation to and by a "further" horizon of intelligibility, one that pointedly extends beyond the self-enclosed naturalism of modernity he terms "the immanent frame." This more expansive horizon, which exceeds the capacity of the immanent frame to articulate fully its philosophical conceptualities, opens an encompassing horizon of further intelligibility—one that may be characterized as a horizon of "abundance" (or even as a horizon of "excess") that can be appropriately and fully demarcated as "theological."

One important consequence of this orientation to a "further" (transcendent) horizon of intelligibility is that Taylor's account does not, as do many modern and post-modern philosophical accounts of the human and its significance, take what has been called "methodological atheism" (or what Taylor calls the "naturalist veto") as an obvious and unarguable starting point. His account neither ignores nor dismisses possibilities that an engagement with questions of transcendence may be at least (conceptually) useful, if not requisite, for articulating an account of the human that provides adequate responses to these two basic anthropological questions. I thus will be further arguing that key coordinates of the conceptual horizon within which Taylor articulates his philosophical anthropology are constituted in reference to long standing articulations of the structures, the activities, and the significance of the human, in which fundamental theological concepts have been historically, culturally, and systematically deeply implicated.

Of these articulations, the workings of "nature" and the workings of "grace," as they bear upon the project of understanding the human and its significance, are among the most historically and systematically important—and, not surprisingly, also are among the most hotly contested ones, both philosophically and theologically. These contestations will not be evaded in the articulations that Taylor elaborates. In fact, I am proposing that the *philosophical* anthropology that Taylor proposes is framed by a presumption that has a strong claim to be characteristically "Catholic" in *both* its *philosophical expression* and its *theological import*. By this I mean that the philosophical account of the human (including the self-understanding of the human as itself a constitutive part of such an account[1]) that Taylor constructs is such that it resists an "either/or" bifurcation of "grace" and of

1 I take the inclusion of self-understanding as itself a fundamental feature of the parsing of the "human" to be one way to articulate the significance of Taylor's affirmation that humans are "self-interpreting" animals; see "Self-interpreting animals," *Human Agency and Language: Philosophical Papers I* (Cambridge: Cambridge University Press, 1985), 45–76.

"nature," as well as a bifurcation of the related conceptual pairing of "faith" and "reason." In Taylor's account these stand constitutively as a (large-and-small "c") Catholic "both/and": They stand in a mutually supportive—even though a sometimes highly contentious—relation to one another in which both contribute to a dynamic of mutual intelligibility that enables exchange to take place between an important range of philosophical and theological idioms.

Locating Taylor's anthropology within a horizon demarcated in reference to nature/grace [faith/reason] coordinately construed, however, carries with it an important *caveat* that is both methodological and substantive. Taylor signals this caveat in a variety of ways, of which I take the most significant to occur in reminders he periodically posts that any adequate understanding of the human must take account of its fully concrete "situatedness." His project's fundamental concern is thus not with abstract forms and renderings of nature and grace, nor of counterpart renderings of reason and faith, but with each of these coordinate pairs (joined to one another, as it were, at their "conceptual and imaginative hips") in the concrete forms they take and are enacted in the world.

Taylor's fundamental anthropological concern is thus with humanity *as it is concretely embodied in conditions of the spatio-temporal finitude of the cosmos and in the social and historical workings of the human cultures in which humanity has emerged.* In philosophical terms, his concern is with an anthropology of what he terms "situated freedom."[2] Such an anthropology of situated freedom, I will propose, provides a central condition of possibility for rendering Taylor's philosophical anthropology open to a theological construal. Such a construal would enable a theological placement of Taylor's anthropology within the dynamics of creation, incarnation, and the sanctification that is the transforming work of the Spirit. The claim advanced here, in sum, is that a theological subtext

2 *Sources of the Self: The Making of the Modern Identity* (Cambridge: Cambridge University Press, 1989), 514–15.

is embedded within Taylor's philosophical anthropology—a subtext that is replete with resonances that draw attention to our creaturely *finitude* and the consequences it bears for our human self-understanding as finite creatures in a finite cosmos.

This finitude, which inhabits our human lives and the conditions of those lives in a multiplicity of forms, is a marker of the radical dependence in which we—and the world in which we dwell and act—stand as created in interdependent relationship to one another.[3] Attention to this *finitude of radical dependence* empowers the self-understanding proper to our human situatedness; it enables us to articulate, for both philosophical and theological anthropology, *loci* from which it becomes possible to acknowledge the radical *contingency* that is the mark of creaturehood. One *locus* for such acknowledgment is in the thoroughgoing *vulnerability* that pervades our embodied condition; a second *locus* is the *fragmentation,* the inner and outer "fractured horizons" of meaning that seem ineluctably to place our capacity to envision and to enact good in an often-isolating dependence upon the will and capacity of *others* to enact good *with* us. Contingency, vulnerability, and fragmentation—singly or in concert with each other—thus mark out key terms of the finitude within which we are called upon to exercise our human freedom. What they each put at stake for our finite freedom is our capacity for exercising that freedom in the *fulness of mutuality—i.e., in function of an unconditional recognition and respect for the other*—to which we are called (and call upon each other) to enact within the conditions of our interdependent finitude.

3 For a related discussion of the Trinitarian character of human freedom, see Philip J. Rossi, "Human Freedom and the Triune God," *T & T Clark Handbook of Theological Anthropology*, ed. Mary Ann Hinsdale and Stephen Oakey (New York: Bloomsbury Publishing, 2021), 123–34. For what I consider to be a classic conceptual and imaginative articulation of the radical dependence that is entailed in the creaturely dependence of creation, see H. Richard Niebuhr, *The Responsible Self: An Essay in Christian Moral Philosophy* (New York: Harper and Row, 1963), especially chapter 4, "Responsibility in Absolute Dependence," 108–26.

Put in more general terms, the finitude of our freedom places us in a relational space of interdependence that calls upon us to recognize and enact our mutuality with others. This recognition and enactment of *mutuality* with one another is an acknowledgement of both the *finitude* of our human freedom and *the solidarity* that issues from *the inherently social character of that freedom*. It is an enactment that properly marks the contingency of the radical human interdependence that constitutes us with one another as an abiding moral community. On Taylor's account, the interdependence of such a moral community provides a key condition of possibility for the attainment of human "fullness," a possibility that exceeds what may be attainable under the dynamic of the isolating interaction of the "buffered selves" locked within the characteristically isolating social imaginaries of the "secular age" of modernity and its aftermath.[4] In theological terms, this recognition of our finitude entails an acknowledgement of the radical contingency of our humanity, a contingency in which we stand in relation to one another, both in the cosmos and within in the workings of history and culture. Our finitude places us in what I term "the conditions of worldly contingency"—such as fragility, vulnerability, incompleteness, and mutual interdependence—from which and in which we are called upon to encounter and respect the "*other*" in *its* own conditions of finite human freedom.

It is within the context of these intersecting dynamics of finitude—interdependence, contingency, vulnerability, fracture, incompleteness, the self-enclosure of "buffered selves"—that we are called upon to exercise our freedom precisely *in its finitude*. It is with reference to these dynamics that Taylor offers elements from which to construct, in the first instance, a philosophical anthropology consonant with our human situatedness within this radical finitude of creaturely dependence. Yet as significant as that construction may be as a philosophical contribution to continued

4 I thus argue, most extensively in chapter 5, that what Immanuel Kant envisions as the abiding human moral community—what he calls a "kingdom of ends"—anticipates in some important respects the social dynamic toward human "fullness" that Taylor articulates.

inquiry in response to the two basic anthropological questions, there is still more to Taylor's project.

What it additionally provides is a basis from which to frame responses to the questions about "the human," to discern and situate the enactments of those *unasked-for altered perspectives and transformations that have power to move us from closure to openness, from rejection to acceptance.* These theology appropriately invites us to see as "grace."[5] In Taylor's account, these enactments are present and offered in "the conditions of worldly contingency," the fractured finite circumstances that, in their distinctive ways, constitute the secular cultures of late modernity and its aftermath. In these finite circumstances, the situatedness of human agency for bringing about good thoroughly pertains to, and is rooted in, a finite human agency embedded in the interdependent workings of contingency.

Our human agency is thus exercised in the fragile circumstances of embodied human vulnerability and fragility that, even as it invites us to deeper mutuality with one another, also has power to divert us to the dead end of a self-enclosure that leads not to mutuality but to the chaos of mutual distrust and hostility. We cannot deny that we each do stand, in the aloneness of our buffered selves, in an embodied condition that seems to provide thin and tenuous protection to our core dignity of spirit. Yet in this precarious condition, our ultimate bulwark against self-enclosure is not to turn against each other. Our real bulwark, rather, is the empowerment of a freely offered and freely accepted mutual recognition of the fragile and vulnerable freedom we each embody and that we are called upon to enact in the welcome of hospitality to one another.

5 See the chapter "Conversions" in *A Secular Age* (Cambridge, MA: Belknap Press of Harvard University Press, 2007)—for a particularly important discussion that Taylor offers of transformations that manifest what is appropriately rendered theologically as the action/effect of "grace." A case can be made that Taylor's discussion here bears important affinities to his discussions of the transformative powers of "epiphanies" in his earlier *Sources of the Self* (418–54, 456–93).

The dynamics of hospitality—and of inhospitality—thus provide a significant trope for encountering the other in the context of worldly contingency and creaturely finitude. It is in our welcoming of the "other"—or in our refusing to offer a welcome—that we enter into the concrete dynamics and challenges of the conditions of worldly contingency; in each case we are called upon to enact and to invite mutual recognition, to encounter *others* in *their own conditions of "worldly contingency"* that provide them with their particular contexts for exercising their finite human freedom. The same dynamic is put in play when the roles are reversed, and we find ourselves as the ones seeking welcome. As George Steiner has sagely noted "we must teach other human beings to be guests to each other."[6] Hospitality offered, hospitality received, may well be an ongoing finite enactment, its social form, of the "original grace" of "the hospitality of God."[7]

ACKNOWLEDGMENTS

Early in the 1990s, the work of Charles Taylor became of interest to me during a sabbatical leave spent at the Institute for Advanced Studies in the Humanities at the University of Edinburgh. That early interest subsequently led to my making two panel presentations on aspects of Taylor's work, one at the 1995 Annual Meeting of the College Theology Society, the other at the 1996 Annual Convention of the Catholic Theological Society of America. Since then, there have been a series of opportunities to make presentations on aspects of Taylor's work, in different venues in the United States and internationally. So, first of all, I would like, to express

6 Quoted by Theo Hobson, "On Being a Perfect Guest": *The Tablet* Interview: George Steiner," *The Tablet* 259 (August 11, 2005): 15.

7 A discussion that locates hospitality in an ecclesial context referenced to the parable of the "wedding feast"/"great feast" as told in the Gospel of Matthew (22: 1–14) and in the Gospel of Luke (14: 16–24) can be found in Philip J. Rossi, SJ, "Sojourners, Guests, and Strangers: The Church as Enactment of the Hospitality of God," *Questions liturgiques—Liturgical Questions* 90, no. 2–3 (2009): 121–31.

my gratitude and appreciation for the encouragement and support I have received during many years of engaging Taylor's work, from faculty colleagues at Marquette University, as well as from students, staff, and college and university administrations.

I also am abidingly grateful for the interest this work has received from colleagues in other parts of the world: these include the members of the Faculty of Systematic Theology at Katholieke Universiteit Leuven, Belgium, who accepted proposals for presentations on Taylor that I submitted for placement on the programs of the biennial gatherings of *Leuven Encounters in Systematic Theology* (LEST), and who also were gracious hosts during a portion of a sabbatical leave in fall 2013. Also deserving of what these days is known as a "shout out" are the members of the faculty in the Philosophy Department of the Ateneo de Manila in the Philippines who hosted me for a semester in the latter part of 1998. I am also deeply grateful to the Council for Research in Values and Philosophy (CRVP) and the McLean Center for the Study of Culture and Values (MCSCV) at The Catholic University of America in Washington, DC. The conferences, seminars, and consultations organized under their auspices (including multi-year, international and interdisciplinary projects on "Faith in Public Life" and on "Renewing the Church in a Secular Age") provided occasions not only for engaging Taylor's thought on the printed pages of his books and essays but also in extended in-person (and, more recently, virtual) conversational exchanges. Many thanks are due here—especially to Charles himself, to William A. Barbieri and Hu Yeping, director and executive director, respectively, of the McLean Center, and most fittingly, to the late Fr. George McLean, OMI (1929–2016), founder of the Council for Research in Values and Philosophy, who even now remains with us as a guiding presence and guardian spirit for the interdisciplinary and cross-cultural work of the Council and the McLean Center.

The list of other colleagues who, in ways large and small, have taken part with me in productive engagement with Taylor's philosophical achievements and/or explored the theological ramifications of his work is far more extensive than can be acknowledged in this short notice. I would, nonetheless, like to conclude with explicit mention and thanks to two colleagues, Dr. Anthony Godzieba, professor emeritus of Theology, Villanova University, Pennsylvania, and Prof. Dr. Markus Wriedt, Faculty of Evangelical Theology, Goethe Universität, Frankfurt-am-Main. Both in conversation and in formal academic presentations, Tony and Markus have, over the course of many years, unfailingly provided me with trenchant insights and provocative analyses that helped me to shape and to refine the claims, the arguments—and the images and tropes—that now constitute this extended essay on the work of Charles Taylor, *Grace and Freedom in a Secular Age.*

Part I

Contingency and the Dynamics of Immanence

Chapter 1

The Pressures of Immanence and the Eclipse of Transcendence

PRELUDES TO AN ANTHROPOLOGY OF GRACE

WHETHER AND HOW HUMAN BEINGS and the cosmos within which they have emerged stand in relation to a transcendent reality has become highly contested in the current era of late modernity that Charles Taylor has termed a "secular age." Long traditions of both reflective thought and religious practice, most prominently in Western culture, have considered such transcendent reality to be divine and providential and have named it personally as "God." In his magisterial works on the rise of secularity, *Sources of the Self* and *A Secular Age*, Taylor has argued that belief in a transcendent, personal, and providential God, which had been the "default position" interwoven into the social imaginary of the dominant Christian culture of the West for more than a millennium,[1] has now become a "contested" option; it is now one of many possibilities on offer for a life orientation, including a

1 He defines a "social imaginary" as "the ways in which [people] imagine their social existence, how they fit together with others, how things go on between them and their fellows, the expectations which are normally met, and the deeper normative notions and images that underlie these expectations." *A Secular Age* (Cambridge, MA: Belknap Press of Harvard University Press, 2007), 171; see also ch. 4, "Modern Social Imaginaries," 159–211, and Charles Taylor, *Modern Social Imaginaries* (Durham, NC: Duke University Press, 2004), for detailed discussions of this concept.

variety of forms of unbelief and non-belief.[2] He argues that this shift has occurred during the course of modernity in consequence of complex sociohistorical processes that have brought about widespread cultural entrenchment of a new social imaginary that altered the enchanted and hierarchical outlook that preceded it. The social imaginary now functioning in our age of secularity, which he terms "the immanent frame," has been constituted by a "constellation" of interlocking cosmic, social, and moral orders of self-sufficient explanation, justification, and practice. Within such an enclosed order of knowing and valuing, belief in God as traditionally understood as personal and providential now has to vie with many other articulations of belief, unbelief, and non-belief. These possibilities form a "nova effect" that opens a seemingly unlimited plurality of pathways, both old and new, for self-understanding and meaning on which individuals and communities may place themselves for the journeys constituting their moral and spiritual lives: "The interesting story [of secularity] is not simply one of the decline [of religion], but also of a new placement of the sacred or the spiritual in relation to individual and social life. The new placement is now the occasion for recompositions of spiritual life in new forms, and for new ways of existing both in and out of relation to God."[3]

Almost two decades before the publication of *A Secular Age*, Taylor had suggested, in *Sources of the Self*, a way to address the

2 The use of both "unbelief" and "non-belief" is intended to signal that in addition to those modes of unbelief that have formed on the basis of explicit rejection of claims about transcendence made on religious or philosophical grounds (such as the modern tradition of atheism as articulated, for instance, in Michael Buckley's *At the Origins of Modern Atheism* [New Haven: Yale University Press, 1987]), there also are forms of "non-belief" for which the possibility of transcendence makes neither theoretical nor practical difference. Unlike classical forms of atheism, which have usually found it necessary to argue for their unbelief, non-belief often functions as a "given" that need not be explicitly justified within contexts of secularity. An important part of the challenge posed by the social imaginary of secularity is that it has provided conditions in which such non-belief becomes unremarkable.

3 Taylor, *A Secular Age*, 437.

circumstances of what he then called the "fractured horizons of modernity" in order to afford "breathing space" to the human spirit.[4] He perceived need for such space to enable us to counter a self-inflicted inattention, even blindness, within those fractured horizons to the deepest moral sources formative of our human self-identity. He framed his suggestion as a need to articulate "anthropologies of situated freedom," a suggestion that stands in strong continuity with the affirmation he has made a number of times during his long intellectual career that its primary focus has been philosophical anthropology—that is, on the questions of what it is to be human and what it means to be human.[5] To a substantial degree, *A Secular Age* provides both the larger lineaments and a rich range of thick description for such an anthropology, which he casts as a multilayered philosophical and historical narrative in which the answers to both questions are shaped in terms of multiple vectors. Among the most important of these vectors is reflective human self-understanding, which undergoes development in the course of history and constitutes us as "self-interpreting animals."[6] Within these vectors are both abiding and mutable factors for orienting human self-understanding, with language having central importance among the abiding ones. The mutable factors arise in the particularities of practices in history, culture, and human social interaction. Their contingent interplay with each other and with human self-understanding articulated

4 Charles Taylor, *Sources of the Self: The Making of the Modern Identity* (Cambridge, MA: Harvard University Press, 1989), 520.

5 See Charles Taylor, "Introduction," in *Human Agency and Language: Philosophical Papers I* (Cambridge: Cambridge University Press, 1985), 1. An early discussion of "situated freedom" can be found in *Hegel* (Cambridge: Cambridge University Press, 1975), 559–71. In the conclusion of a more recent work, *The Language Animal: The Full Shape of the Human Linguistic Capacity* (Cambridge, MA: Harvard University Press, 2016), 338, he proposes that an appropriate reinterpretation of Aristotle's definition of the human being as "rational animal" (*Zwon echon logon*) would be "animal possessing language."

6 See Charles Taylor, "Self-Interpreting Animals," in *Human Agency and Language*, 45–76.

in language provides the concrete and often recalcitrant material from which responses to these fundamental anthropological questions need to be shaped.

While the text of *A Secular Age* shows a skillful grasp of a range of key theological issues that are embedded in his account of these vectors as they function with respect to each other as human cultures unfold, Taylor locates his enterprise as a philosophical work. As such, it is attentive to the methodological and the substantive distinctions, such as the one between "faith" and "reason" that, in Western intellectual history, has historically delimited the scope of each enterprise and the dynamics of their relations to each other. Yet, even as he articulates his arguments and the anthropology embedded in it in a philosophical idiom, it is one that bears the tonality of what, since at least the Reformation, has been a characteristically Catholic presumption that "the human" is such that faith and reason stand in a mutually supportive—even though sometimes contentious—relation to each other.[7] This stands in contrast to a variety of other philosophical and theological views, from a variety of historical provenances (including ones that antedate the Reformation), that place faith and reason in dialectical and even contradictory contrast to each other and to the ways they each enter into the constitution of the "human."

Taylor's work, particularly as exemplified in *Sources of the Self* and *A Secular Age*, also bears upon another theological relationship that functions in congruence with that between faith and reason: the relation/distinction between "nature" and "grace."

7 For an astute reading of how Taylor negotiates the conceptual and lived space between faith and reason in terms of an implicit "theological humanism," see William Schweiker, "Human Flourishing and the Question of Fullness," in *Aspiring for Fullness in Secular Age: Essays on Religion and Theology in the Work of Charles Taylor*, ed. Carlos D. Colorado and Justin D. Classen (Notre Dame, IN: University of Notre Dame Press, 2014), 127–51. See also Charles Taylor, *Avenues of Faith: Conversations with Jonathan Guilbault*, trans. Yvette Shalter (Waco, TX: Baylor University Press, 2020), a set of interviews in which Taylor is asked to reflect upon dimensions of his own faith as a Catholic.

A strong case can be made that these two works of Taylor's, when read in conjunction with each other, constitute an extended effort to frame a philosophical anthropology that is fundamentally oriented to a horizon that can be theologically demarcated in reference to the relationship and the interworking of nature and grace. Of particular importance for discerning the ways this theological distinction comes into play within the philosophical coordinates of his anthropological project is his identification of the "spiritual" as a constitutive element *both* for what it *is* to be human and for *how we then construe our own humanity*—that is, our *self-understanding* of our "being human."[8] In other words, Taylor's anthropology affirms that we are constituted as spiritual *both in our very humanity*—that is, "ontologically,"—*and also in the dynamisms and activities of self-understanding* in which we "reflexively" appropriate our humanity.[9] His philosophical construal of the spiritual as constitutive of our humanity thus offers a basis from which to articulate the relationship between nature and grace theologically: *Our humanity, in the dynamism and activities that constitute it as spiritual, is receptively oriented* to being performatively transformed for, and into, a human wholeness that is *beyond our capacity, individually or communally, for self-enactment*; in other words, our humanity is oriented to being "graced."[10]

---

8 For further discussion, see Philip J. Rossi, SJ, "Divine Transcendence and the 'Languages of Personal Resonance': The Work of Charles Taylor as a Resource for Spirituality in an Era of Post-modernity," in *Theology and Conversation*, ed. J. Haers and P. DeMey (Leuven: Peeters, 2004), 783–94.

9 In terms of Taylor's categories, the overarching term for such reflexive self-appropriation of our humanity is that we are "self-interpreting" animals (see note 6, earlier). In terms of a philosophical anthropology framed in Aristotelian-Thomist categories, instances of the dynamisms that provide reflexive appropriation of our humanity can be located in activities such as the exercise of conscience and judgments of truth, good, and beauty.

10 Readers familiar with the theology of Karl Rahner might recognize this as an articulation concerned with the dynamics of human finitude in relation to God, for which Rahner employs the terminology of "obediential potency" and the "supernatural existential." For a useful discussion of

This has a twofold import for Taylor's anthropology. On one hand, this deeply receptive orientation to the workings of grace is one he considers to be properly denominated philosophically as "spirit." His anthropology may thus be considered one that takes our humanity to be constituted as enfleshed spirit, a claim that anthropologies of reductive naturalism would fiercely resist.[11] On the other hand, he sees that there are dynamics within the immanent frame that have allowed and even promoted modes of narrowed self-understanding that allow us to distract and even to blind ourselves precisely to this profoundly spiritual dimension that is fundamental to the constitution of what and who we are as human. Starkly put, Taylor's account suggests that the demise of the spiritual in human life is more likely to come from self-inflicted wounds brought about by inattention and neglect of its movements within us than by focused and willful intent to uproot it—an ancient possibility that continues to lurk within the immanent frame. His project is thus keyed to drawing our reflective intent and attention back to the deeply rooted activities of spirit that, even amid the distractions and resistances embedded in the immanent fame, continue to empower our self-understanding.

It is my hope that the work that follows will provide a small supplement to Taylor's anthropology by making explicit what I perceive to be important theological implications that arise from his philosophical efforts "to bring the air back into the

---

the two latter terms that places them in the context of their use by Rahner and by Bernard Lonergan, see Jeremy Blackwood, "Lonergan and Rahner on the Natural Desire to See God," *Method*, n.s. 1, no. 2 (2010): 85–103.

11 Transposed into the language of a long tradition of theological anthropology, Taylor's project can be read as an effort to provide a contemporary philosophical grammar with which to parse an affirmation that body and soul, flesh and spirit, are mutually constitutive of human persons. It is of both substantive and methodological import that this grammar is *not* primarily structured in reference to the Thomistic categories that have had abiding influence upon much of Catholic theology's parsing of that same affirmation.

half-collapsed lungs of the spirit."[12] Taylor's work will thus serve as major interlocutor in my effort to articulate initial contours for a theological anthropology that will help to situate and discern the workings of grace in the human circumstances that constitute the cultures of late modernity and its aftermath. My main goal is not, however, to deploy a full-scale theological anthropology elaborated in systemic detail. It is, rather, to provide a set of pertinent glosses offered in theological support of Taylor's philosophical case that we need "anthropologies of situated freedom" that provide space for a robust reflective self-understanding of the working of the human spirit in the fractured landscape of meaning and human purpose that marks the aftermath of modernity. These glosses are offered as pointers indicative of how a philosophical anthropology of the kind Taylor explores may serve as a fitting "prolegomenon" for theological understandings of grace appropriate to the fragmented cultures of meaning for which the term "postmodernity" often stands as signpost.

I will thus argue that framing an anthropology that is explicitly situated in reference to what Taylor terms the "fractured horizons" of meaning that are the legacy of modernity may prove useful in constructing a theology of grace for these times of secularity. In such a theology of grace, close attention needs to be paid to the fragmentation that deeply marks so many of the modes of human life, meaning, and aspiration, and in which the very exercise of human freedom is now increasingly immersed. Such attention is crucial in that the self-enclosed explanatory dynamics of the immanent frame often take it as given that the fractured horizons of our human circumstance necessarily and decisively count against discerning anything that might legitimately be considered "grace": These horizons provide neither conceptual nor imaginative space for sense and purpose that may be other than whatever can be rendered intelligible in terms of those self-enclosed dynamics. For the immanent frame, there

12 Taylor, *Sources of the Self*, 520.

is no larger "horizon" of meaning or purpose from which to frame an account of our humanity or of its role in the course of the world. The only possibilities for meaning and purpose are those presented or extracted from the self-enclosed explanatory dynamics of the immanent frame. For such a world of irremediably shattered meanings there can be, in consequence, no events, persons, relations, nor circumstances with a capacity to disclose *the workings of a transcendent other, a presence to which our humanity may be ordered in its finitude*, that points to horizons of sense and purpose ampler than those provided by the fractured spaces of the immanent frame.

The immanent frame thus takes the range of sense and meaning that can be articulated in response to the anthropological questions of what it is to be human and what it means to be human to be a function of the "fractured horizons" of meaning that are the legacy of modernity. These horizons are construed to have no space—be it conceptual or ontological—for grace and/or transcendence to be operative and, a fortiori, to be discerned. In contrast to this depiction of human meaning as inevitably self-enclosed, a condition that he terms "stifling,"[13] Taylor offers a reading of these circumstances that, even as it recognizes the scope of the fracturing of sense and meaning they bring in their wake, challenges the adequacy of taking self-enclosure and reductive intelligibility as an exhaustive rendering of the trope of the "immanent frame."

Taylor provides, instead, the lineaments of an anthropology that enables us to articulate our fractured human circumstances, not as an inevitably recursive self-enclosure, but as the conditions of worldly contingency in which we are called upon to "encounter the *other* in its condition of freedom."[14] These circumstances do

---

13 Taylor, *Sources of the Self*, 520: "We have read so many goods out of our official story, we have buried their power so deep beneath layers of philosophical rationale, that they are in danger of stifling. Or rather, since they are our goods, human goods, *we* are stifling."

14 The expression is from George Steiner, *Real Presences* (Chicago: University of Chicago Press, 1989), 4. He goes on to argue that such an account of freedom with freedom constitutes "a wager on transcendence."

not inevitably testify to a chaotic darkness from which there is no exit, ineluctably ending in the unrelieved absence or the adamant refusal of any possibility of grace. They are, rather, powerful and variegated invitations to recognize, in encountering the disorienting otherness of fracture in our circumstances and also in ourselves, a "gracing" that invites our participation in the performance of wholeness. Their "darkness" is one that keeps watch for the fire of God's Spirit to ignite the rich kindling of the human spirit that, in the very otherness of the darkness in which it lies, has already been primed by that same Spirit to burst into flames, illuminating the ever-expansive reach of God's love. Taylor's rendering of the very circumstances of secularity as crucial loci for discerning *grace performed in encountering otherness* thus may help make it possible to discern that Spirit at work even in the "nova effect," the multiplicity of contested and adamantly fractured options for belief, unbelief, and non-belief that Taylor identifies as a major transformative outcome of secularity.

As rich as Taylor's work is for helping to sketch a theological anthropology indexed to the work of grace, he will not be the sole interlocutor for this project, particularly with respect to describing the lineaments and the limits of the "immanent frame" of the cultures of secularity. The work of both Susan Neiman and George Steiner, which I take to represent an important current in secular thought that is attentive and attuned to the dimensions of the human that Taylor identifies as "spirit," provides an important supplement to Taylor's account. Their work is of particular import for this effort to articulate the theological resonances issuing from the philosophical account of the human that Taylor provides inasmuch as it is articulated in a philosophical mode that is keenly alert to human finitude and the strictures it places upon both philosophical and theological discourse and conceptuality. In counterpoint to Taylor's carefully framed adherence to a general congruence in the workings of faith and reason that resonates with a principle that has long been characteristic of Catholic theology, neither Neiman nor Steiner endorses such congruence as a starting point. At the same time, neither do they place themselves in alliance with those strands of modernity and secularity that consider it pointless to undertake efforts to find bases to make their mutual engagement possible. They keep the possibility of such engagement on the table even as they are reticent, to a point bordering upon the apophatic, with respect to human capacities for positively characterizing as transcendent that "other" over against which the contours of human self-understanding and agency take their contingent and finite shape. The congruence that Taylor takes here as given—at least methodologically—is one that Neiman and Steiner take as, at least in the first instance, a problem and a project. It is a problem and a project, moreover, that they both see of major importance for the possibility of framing a sound response to the core anthropological questions: "what it is to be human" and "what it means to be human." In this regard, they stand on common ground with Taylor. They all are cognizant that in some fundamental way the grammar of the finitude that constitutes us as human—and thereby enables us to characterize "what it is to be human"—is a function of the intelligibility we also are invited to articulate for a grammar of transcendence—that is, a grammar of the "other" over against which we stand in our finitude.

AUTONOMY RECONFIGURED:
THE DIGNITY AND THE FRAGILITY OF FREEDOM

In addition to these contemporary interlocutors, there is a figure of major significance in the intellectual culture of modernity whose work will play a key role in delimiting the anthropological contours in which I will argue that the workings of grace within the immanent frame may be discerned: Immanuel Kant. To those familiar with the role that Kant is often assigned in the emergence of modernity, his thought would appear to go significantly counter to an enterprise seeking to render the workings of grace intelligible for the secular cultures that are modernity's offspring. Kant's legacy is most commonly taken to have significantly shaped the trajectory of "The Enlightenment" in placing strictures upon the possibility for cognizing God and in giving human autonomy a central place in the moral order informing secularity. This influential interpretation of Kant—which I will term an immanentist account—gives greatest weight to his epistemic concerns and takes his most significant legacy to be the dismantling of metaphysics, particularly with respect to claims to yield knowledge of any transcendent reality.[15] Concomitant with this is the establishing of the autonomy of individual agents, in an apparent zero-sum relationship with the agency of God, as the central feature of the human moral world. Over against this immanentist interpretation, I will be arguing that there is "another Kant" whose thought offers major resources for constructive theological engagement on the manner in which humans participate in the enactment of grace.[16] This is a Kant whose intellectual configuration has emerged out of recent interpretive studies of elements of his work that have recovered his attentiveness to the social character of the finite reason that humans exercise. These studies point to conceptual resources in his work that are of consequence for elaborating an anthropology of situated freedom that stands open to the transcendent in and for this time of secularity. The most pertinent of these resources can be found in his account of our finite human moral agency that, inasmuch as it is embedded in a human social relationality sustained in the mutuality of moral hope, helps to shape the trajectory of human history within the workings of the cosmos.

These studies thus significantly reposition the focus of Kant's work and the import of its legacy. This other Kant did not configure his critical project, as the immanentist account

15 This "epistemic" construal of Kant is part of a larger hermeneutic of the history of modern philosophy and intellectual culture that has made the inquiries and methods of the physical sciences the paradigm of cognitive access to the real. Its most stringent expression can be found in what will be examined later as the "naturalistic" presuppositions that are embedded in the social imaginary of the immanent frame.

16 I have used the expression "another Kant" to echo the title of an important collection of essays by Aloysius Winter, *Der andere Kant: Zur philosophische Theologie Immanuel Kants* (Hildesheim: Olms, 2000).

would have it, primarily out of a preoccupation with either epistemological issues raised by the Cartesian turn to the subject or challenges to Newtonian science arising from the radical empiricism of Hume. Though these concerns played a role in his enterprise, the primary and sustained thrust of his thinking concerned, instead, the proper construal of the uniquely finite, embodied, and social form in which reason functions as a constitutive element of the human in its moral engagement with the world. On this reading, Kant's project is at root anthropological, focused on grappling with the question "What is the human?" This is the question he explicitly acknowledges as unifying the three questions posed in the *Critique of Pure Reason*—"What can I know?" "What ought I do?" and "What may I hope for?"—that jointly express the interests driving the dynamics of finite human reason in our cognitive and moral engagements with the world.[17]

This repositioning of the focus of Kant's critical philosophy to the anthropological has a specific bearing upon my effort to outline the contours of a theological anthropology of situated freedom from which to discern the workings of grace in the immanent frame of secularity. These recent studies of Kant have helped to build a case for understanding his philosophical rendering of the role of human finite reason in our engagement of the world to include—and perhaps even to rest upon—a far more robust understanding of our human cosmic and social situatedness than has previously been recognized.[18] This can be most

17 He poses these three question in the *Critique of Pure Reason* A 805/B 833; the question about the human is found in the *Lectures on Logic* (*Akademie Ausgabe* 9:25) and in a letter to C. F. Stäudlin, May 4, 1793 (*Akademie Ausgabe* 11:429).

18 In addition to the essays by Aloysius Winter noted above, see, for instance, Sharon Anderson Gold, *Unnecessary Evil* (Albany: State University of New York Press, 2001); Patrick Frierson, *Freedom and Anthropology in Kant's Moral Philosophy* (Cambridge: Cambridge University Press, 2003); Jeanine Grenberg, *Kant and the Ethics of Humility: A Story of Dependence, Corruption and Virtue* (Cambridge: Cambridge University Press, 2005);

notably seen in the development of his fully mature account of the workings of human moral agency. In contrast, for instance, to an almost exclusive stress on formal and deontological elements in Kant's account of the maxims governing an individual agent's moral choice, more recent studies take note of Kant's placement of these accounts in texts that attend to the concrete lineaments of ordinary human moral life. They give weight to the fact that crucial points of his arguments draw support, not from an abstract rendering of rationality, but from direct appeal to such things as "the common idea of duty and moral laws," "natural sound understanding," "the common human reason," and "the moral cognition of common human reason."[19] These discussions of moral agency are marked by a deep respect for the humanity in every individual, whatever his or her status or condition in society, which originated in Kant's reading of Rousseau.[20] They are equally marked by an awareness that the exercise of human moral agency is fully embedded in a social relationality that takes its full moral form as membership in a reciprocally ordered "kingdom of ends."

Susan Neiman, *Evil in Modern Thought: An Alternative History of Philosophy* (Princeton: Princeton University Press, 2002); Susan Neiman, *The Unity of Reason: Rereading Kant* (New York: Oxford University Press, 1994); Robert Louden, *Kant's Impure Ethics: From Rational Beings to Human Beings* (New York: Oxford University Press, 2000); G. Felicitas Munzel, *Kant's Conception of Moral Character* (Chicago: University of Chicago Press, 1999); Philip J. Rossi, SJ, *The Social Authority of Reason* (Albany: State University of New York Press, 2005); Philip J. Rossi, SJ, *The Ethical Commonwealth in History: Peace-Making as the Moral Vocation of Humanity* (Cambridge: Cambridge University Press, 2019); Holly L. Wilson, *Kant's Pragmatic Anthropology* (Albany: State University of New York Press, 2006).

19 Immanuel Kant, *Groundwork of the Metaphysics of Morals* (G), trans. Mary J. Gregor, in *Practical Philosophy: The Cambridge Edition of the Works of Immanuel Kant*, ed. Paul Guyer and Allen W. Wood (Cambridge: Cambridge University Press, 1996), 44, 52, 57, 58; Immanuel Kant, *Grundlegung zur Metaphysik der Sitten*, in *Kants Gesammelte Schriften* (Berlin: Königlich Preussischen Akademie der Wissenschaften, 1902), 5:389, 397, 402, 403.

20 Manfred Kuehn, *Kant: A Biography* (Cambridge: Cambridge University Press, 2001), 131–32.

In the context of the larger trajectory of Kant's critical philosophy, his discussions of moral agency thus provide one key marker indicating that his project's fundamental concern is not with an abstract form of reason, but with reason in the concrete form it takes in a humanity embodied in conditions of spatio-temporal finitude and the social and historical workings of human culture. On these accounts, the critical project is thoroughly anthropological; it is concerned with the unique position human beings occupy in the cosmos as the juncture of nature and freedom and, in accord with that status, also concerned with the vocation of humanity to bring about, in a manner appropriate to the exercise of finite reason, the social and cultural conditions under which freedom and nature may work together for the attainment of "the highest good" for all of humanity. This anthropological focus helps to provide the concrete coordinates to the primacy that Kant assigns to the practical use of reason in service of humanity's moral vocation.

One consequence of this anthropological reading of Kant is that it helps to dislodge an influential understanding of "autonomy" from what has long been implicitly presumed to be its conceptual "home": the dynamics of a social (and cosmic) atomism that has itself been formative of the moral order of the immanent frame. In contrast to this reading of Kant's account of the autonomy of our agency, which is at once strongly individualist and highly abstract, I will propose an alternative account in which *autonomy is embedded in the mutual recognition agents accord one another as equal participants in a moral community*, a recognition that is expressed in practices of social respect.[21] The crucial bearing that this shift will have upon the contours of theological anthropology is that it offers a basis for a construal of the relationship of human moral autonomy to faith empowered by grace that is quite different from the zero-sum account that has

21 This way of reading autonomy cuts against the grain of certain philosophical renderings of "modernity" and "secularity," even before referencing it theologically to a horizon of faith.

typically been a constitutive element in the immanent frame; that construal is one that pits the human freedom of moral agents in competition both with one another's freedom, in the manner of a Hobbesian "state of nature," and with the divine freedom in which the grace enabling faith is offered.

In accord with this proposed social reading of autonomy, I will indicate how faith, understood as a transformative seeing enabled by grace, may be appropriately understood as an affirmation of an order of transcendence that makes possible, rather than contravenes, the robust exercise of human finite moral agency. In the context of this affirmation, faith offers to the structure and the workings of autonomous moral agency a formative social context that is fitting for moral engagement with a secular age; this social context is of particular import for addressing the ways in which the workings of secularity have made manifest how thoroughly our humanity is enmeshed in and thus deeply vulnerable to the fracturing interplay of contingency. The formative social context that faith provides encompasses a robust sense of human social and historical responsibility as it is exercised in view of a graced horizon of hope. It provides a basis for affirming a fundamental moral priority for the role of *humanity, as a mutually interrelated whole*, in shaping the social and cultural history that forms the distinctively human mode of interaction with the cosmos.[22] Acknowledging divine transcendence thus fully affirms human moral responsibility for shaping the direction of history and culture, in contrast to the way the immanent frame frequently construes transcendence and human moral responsibility as locked in zero-sum competition.

This recasting of Kant's account of autonomy into an anthropological register that recognizes the constitutive embedding of human moral agency in a matrix of social and historical relationality has an additional consequence for the contours of the account

---

22 One indication of this repositioning within Kant's work is that, as the critical project moves into the 1790s, his discussion of hope shifts focus from personal immortality toward the final outcome of humanity's career as a species.

of human situatedness I am proposing. One kernel of truth in the immanentist account is that it affirms the deep connection Kant makes between autonomy as the exercise of human moral freedom and the recognition of the dignity of the human person. This connection has played an important role in framing the discourse of the human rights through which modernity articulates a key dimension of our humanity. A correspondingly important feature of Kant's account of dignity that an immanentist reading frequently fails to notice, however, is how his recognition of the inestimable dignity of the power of human freedom to effect good is also a recognition that such power resides in agents who are profoundly fragile, particularly in the face of the natural and social circumstances in which they are called upon to exercise that freedom. The human power for bringing good to be in freedom thoroughly pertains to, and is rooted in, a finite practical reason that is exercised in the fragile circumstances of embodied human vulnerability. In the absence of the recognition of such vulnerability, even a discourse as morally powerful as that of human rights can be ineffectual in providing a sufficiently encompassing sense of the dignity that arises from our human mutuality and our solidarity in responsibility for one another.[23]

It is thus Kant's recognition of both the dignity *and* the fragility of human finite freedom that provides the bases upon which his account of human agency will serve as one of the constitutive elements in the anthropological account I am proposing. His affirmation of human dignity represents one major feature of the social character of human autonomy that I will argue is a locus for the graced empowering of human agents to be effective participants in the ordering of history; such ordering is one that moves along a trajectory toward human fullness that, even though inscribed in and throughout the abounding gratuity of

23 This is a line of criticism that Taylor has framed (*Sources of the Self*, 53–75) in terms of modernity's "inarticulacy" with respect to its "moral sources" of justice and benevolence, an inarticulacy that ironically blocks those sources from fully empowering our moral agency for meeting the high moral demands they place on us.

creation, is nonetheless only fitfully glimpsed from the vulnerable circumstances of our finitude. Kant's affirmation of the fragility that marks the agency with which we exercise our finite freedom represents the other side of that same empowering. In fact, on his account, the fragility of human freedom stands coordinate to its dignity: As we each stand alone, our embodied state provides thin and tenuous protection to our core dignity of spirit; its ultimate bulwark is mutual recognition, the respect we accord one another for the fragile and vulnerable freedom we each embody.

It is on the basis of this mutual interrelation between the fragility and the dignity of human freedom within a horizon of a shared human mutuality that Kant articulates his account of the rational hope that gives shape to the moral vocation incumbent on us all. Such hope empowers us to engage one another in ways enabling us to establish social conditions effective for securing the "highest good," not simply for one's individual self, but for humanity as a whole. In keeping with the tropes of the "ethical commonwealth" and a "kingdom of ends" that he uses to designate the context for attaining this good, this is a good that itself is robustly social. In more concrete terms, Kant takes such hope to provide a basis from which human beings can sustain one another in efforts to provide the social conditions that will make possible a cosmopolitan international order that will bring about lasting peace among the nations and peoples of the world.

Within the anthropological framework that Kant articulates, human mutuality thus provides the context for affirming a social hope based on the dignity and fragility of human freedom. The focus that Kant then places upon the central importance of working for peace—it is morally imperative for *all* humanity— is one that I will propose bears special weight with respect to the possibility of providing a basis for substantive theological engagement with the fracturing dynamics of a secular age. This import, however, has less to do with a commonly accepted interpretation of the cosmopolitan world order Kant proposes as a secularization of the scriptural trope of "the kingdom of God." It has more to do, instead, with the way he articulates the conditions that enable humanity to take individual and mutual responsibility with one another for the trajectory of history. On Kant's account this is a task that can be fully engaged and sustained only to the extent that it is done in recognition that our finitude places limits on the effectiveness of our human power to bring that history to its morally appropriate final completion.

This recognition of our historical finitude with respect to the social character of our human moral vocation provides a further marker for our human situatedness that helps to locate how humanity stands in relation to divine transcendence. In theological terms, entailed in this recognition of finitude is an acknowledgment of the radical contingency in which we stand in the cosmos and in the workings of history. Recognition of the finitude from which we are called upon to enact our responsibility for both the trajectory of history and the space of the cosmos in which we dwell opens a horizon of hope that entrusts its completion to the working of an agency not in our power to control, an agency that Kant variously calls "nature" or "providence."[24] In this, Kant affirms that within the recognition of our moral finitude and the responsibility for one another that it places upon us there is also recognition of the fragility of our situatedness with respect to our role in the eschatological completion of history: In Kant's terminology, full engagement of our moral efforts, undertaken in awareness of our finitude, "postulates" in hope their final completion through an agency that is not ours.

I will thus be arguing that the interrelation between the fragility and the dignity of human freedom, as it is placed within the horizon of a shared human mutuality, is crucial not just to Kant's overall account of our human moral vocation. This relation between human fragility and human dignity also helps to locate key coordinates from which an anthropology of situated freedom can delineate the contours of hope requisite for sustaining our human spiritual and moral vocation in our own times of secularity. This hope, moreover, shows itself to be even more encompassing in its scope than is the rational hope that Kant proposed as integral to our human moral vocation. Kant was quite aware of the deep fissures of meaning and intentionality that run all the way down in the constitution of our humanity, even to a point that Susan Neiman refers to it as "a metaphysic of permanent rupture."[25] Yet it is at least arguable that, on his account, the fractures in his context that ran athwart the work of constituting a kingdom of ends were, in retrospect, less pervasive and extensive than those we now perceive upon the landscape of fragmented possibilities, broken meaning, and thwarted intention with which the immanent frame of secularity has circumscribed what Taylor terms our deepest human aspirations. On this more deeply fractured landscape, Kant's account of the mutuality of our finite moral agency points us toward a horizon of hope, though it does not by itself offer all the coordinates needed to orient our journey upon our present landscape. Another of these requisite coordinates will be indicated as we take steps to locate, beginning in the next section, the exercise of our human moral agency within the workings of the encompassing contingencies of creation: Our finite freedom stands in a space of mutuality that properly marks the contingency of radical dependence that constitutes us as part of a creation.

CONTINGENCY, OTHERNESS, AND THE GRACIOUSNESS OF GOD'S HOSPITALITY

The relocating of human moral agency within the context of social relationality thus will provide a key marker for the contours of a theological anthropology of situated freedom. It will be on the basis of this marker that it will be possible to discern, from within the fractured landscapes and horizons of the immanent frame, the space from which hope beckons us to exercise our capacities to

25 Neiman, *Evil in Modern Thought*, 80.

bring human wholeness out of such fracture. The aim of this hope is, first, to sustain our engagement with one another in full recognition of our mutuality in its fragility and its dignity and, second, to enact that hope effectively for one another's abiding good and for the good of the cosmos in which we dwell. It will thus not be the main purpose of this account of hope as it is resituated within human mutuality to provide a new or substantially different description of the fracture that lies upon the well-traversed landscape of modernity. To a large degree, the maps that provide the most helpful guides for orientation along the route my account will take are those drawn by (among others) Taylor, Neiman, and Steiner; these maps have pointed out the location of the deepest and most enduring fractures that, even as they make precarious the human terrain on which we dwell with one another, also invite a respectful—and possibly healing—engagement with that very precariousness for which Neiman and Steiner each employ telling and poignant tropes: "attention to the pieces" (Neiman) and the "tact of heart" that Steiner calls *cortesia*.[26]

My account will indicate how the work of these authors offers coordinates for navigating the fractured terrain of the aftermath of modernity not, as secularity would have it, within a landscape enclosing us in the limiting self-referential horizons of an immanent frame; the philosophical coordinates that Taylor, Neiman, and Steiner provide serve, instead, as points of reference that make it possible to locate the often fragile features, which are easy to overlook or to disdain, on this fractured landscape that invite attention and openness to the transforming power that theology names "grace." They do so, I will be arguing, by enabling us to situate this landscape, fractured as it may be, in reference to the contexts of contingency in which our human finitude and vulnerability render us open to transforming hope.

Fundamental to these contexts is what I will delimit subsequently, in more detail, as a twofold contingency that encompasses our human circumstances of finitude in its interplay. This interplay

---

26 Neiman, *Evil in Modern Thought*, 326; Steiner, *Real Presences*, 146–50.

renders our mutual human vulnerability not, as the immanent frame would have it, as an indication of the absence of grace, another feature of a worldly order at best indifferent to human aspirations and purposes. The account to be given here, woven in the first instance from the (mostly) philosophical strands provided variously by Taylor, Neiman, Steiner, and Kant, will elaborate a different, more hopeful, articulation of our human situatedness in its vulnerability to contingency. In this articulation, the twofold interplay of contingency upon our finitude provides a space from which it becomes possible to discern our very vulnerability to contingency as itself a fundamental locus for discerning the workings of a transforming grace in these times of secularity.

The further articulation of this context, which has theological as well as philosophical inflections, will draw upon the contributions that both David Burrell and Robert Sokolowski have made to parsing the "grammar" of creation. On their account, the radical otherness that distinguishes the Creator, as originary, from the entirety of creation that the Creator brings forth and sustains as created otherness provides the fundamental syntax for the ordering of creation. *The otherness of creation itself* exhibits and underlines the sheer gratuity—the "gracing"—with which God brings the finite otherness of creation to be in its entirety. This most radical contingency of creation—that it need not have been at all—can thus be taken to be grace in its first enactment: creation is "original grace."

I will then propose to link this theological account of the contingency that is embedded in the original grace of creation to the philosophical account of a "metaphysic of permanent rupture" that Neiman, in her work on Kant, provides as a central conceptual locus for situating human freedom. I will argue that these two accounts, when read together, offer a way to understand how the two "inflections" of contingency at work in the fractured and fracturing dynamics of secularity's immanent frame then converge upon our shared human vulnerability in a way that makes that vulnerability a primary locus for discerning the presence and working of grace. We are, in the first instance, vulnerable in terms of the contingency that marks the radical dependence of creation upon the "original grace" of God's enacting and sustaining all creation into its being as other than God. This vulnerability is evoked in the recognition that we might not have been at all and, indeed, that creation need not have been at all: The very otherness of creation is radically contingent in its dependence. This is the vulnerability of standing before an abyss of not-being, a vertiginous marker of the radical dependence inscribed in our being creatures. We are, in the second instance, vulnerable in terms of the workings of what I will term "the contingency of uncertain outcome" in creation, the contingency of "what could have been otherwise." This is an inflection of contingency that bears upon both the complex dynamics of our self-understanding and the multileveled materiality of our embodied selves as we are enmeshed in the working of nature, history, and culture and as this enmeshment lays bare the depths of our human vulnerabilities.

I will thus argue that attention to this interplay of contingency, particularly as it requires us to attend to our mutual human vulnerabilities, is central for framing a theological anthropology that gives an account of the human that is adequate to the fragility and the dignity of our human freedom as it engages the fracturing dynamics of "a secular age." Such attention will make it possible to render intelligible the possibility of humanity standing in relation to a transcendent God, even as it is immersed within "secularities" that have both constituted an "immanent frame" for self-understanding and energized a "nova effect" for the human spirit. It will thus be by reference to the interplay of contingency with human vulnerability that such an anthropology will be able to take account of the forces operative in the secularities of late modernity that place efforts to understand the human into a matrix of what Taylor describes as "cross-pressures"; these are forces that "fragilize" what had hitherto been deeply stable zones of explanation and meaning—including, ironically, the very zones of meaning that constitute secularity.[27] On one side,

27 Taylor, *A Secular Age*, 594–617.

there is pressure to reshape our understanding of what makes us human into contours provided by an immanent frame in which God is (presumed) absent but human spiritual impulses continue; on another side, there is pressure on believers to refashion their theological understanding of how the divine gifting that enacts the immanent presence of the transcendent God toward humanity and all creation—an enactment that Christian theology names "grace"—functions with respect to a spiritually restive humanity now dwelling within an "immanent frame."

This account will also draw attention to two important ways in which the perspective of the immanent frame has shaped human engagement with the workings of contingency as it impinges upon our vulnerability. The first is in secularity's assignment of instrumental reason to serve as the locus for human efforts to bring contingency under control; the second is its correlate securing of the identity of the self from the vicissitudes of contingency by disengaging it from the very social relationality that constitutes the finitude of our human freedom.[28] The first context, that of instrumental reason, will be articulated as a central element in the "naturalistic veto" that rises from the operative assumptions of the self-enclosed explanatory dynamics that constitute what Taylor calls the "immanent frame." The second context will be provided by Taylor's account of the "fragilization" of identity within the immanent frame that has made porous many of the boundaries of meaning and practice that once delimited spaces for dwelling in secure possession of our identities. This makes possible an awareness of how deeply the mutuality of our freedom already inscribes the "other" within the ambit of our identity—to the point that we can understand our own identity and agency to be constituted in "immanent otherness." This space of otherness, as later considerations will elaborate, provides a key social locus from which a graced hope, arising from the recognition of the

28 In Taylor's terminology, this disengagement from social relationality is a fundamental feature of the way in which "the buffered self" stands situated in the immanent frame of modernity. See Taylor, *Sources of the Self*, 159–76, *A Secular Age*, 300–21.

mutual vulnerability in which we stand upon the fractured terrain of secularity, empowers possibilities for us to be participant in the healing of fracture.

An important link between these two contexts, of secularity's valuing of instrumental reason and of the fragilization of identity, will then be provided in terms of the complementary tropes—that of being "homeless" and that of being a "guest"—that Neiman and Steiner respectively offer to characterize the circumstances of humanity's dwelling within the immanent frame.[29] Both images will then offer a way to view "fragilization" as creating possibilities for a new awareness of our mutual vulnerabilities in the face of the other—including the other that is within us in the very constitution of our agency. I will propose that these mutual human vulnerabilities offer a primary locus for enactments of grace in times of secularity: This grace is the enactment of a hope that is empowered by the interrelation between the fragility and the dignity of human moral freedom and that takes the form of an inclusive hospitality that both welcomes and accompanies otherness in all its forms and in all its vulnerable precariousness.[30]

The cross-pressures that Taylor sees operative in and upon the immanent frame result in a phenomenon he terms a "fragilization" affecting even the most entrenched and cherished world-perspectives in response to the workings of an immanent frame that seeks to encompass them.[31] As Taylor describes it, fragilization is a phenomenon rooted in dynamics by which the "strangeness" of a worldview inhabited by the religious "other"—including the secularized other of unbelief and of non-belief—no longer stands as "really inconceivable" for me, in part because the cultures of modernity have lessened the

29 Neiman, *Evil in Modern Thought*, 308; Steiner, *Real Presences*, 165–78.

30 For an illuminating theological treatment of vulnerability and precarity, see James F. Keenan, SJ, "The World at Risk: Vulnerability, Precarity, and Connectedness," *Theological Studies* 81, no. 1 (2020): 132–49.

31 See Taylor, *A Secular Age*, 303–4, 531–32.

differences of other kinds between us. The religious other—and even the nonreligious other—has become "more and more like me, in everything else but faith. Then the issue posed by difference becomes more insistent: why my way and not hers?"[32] On Taylor's account fragilization affects us all by creating spaces of uncertain or occluded meaning that unsettle the closure that constitutes the buffered identity of modernity's punctual self. In consequence, fragilization affects not only the religious believer but also those immersed in the modes of secularity that locate the human completely within a closed world order of self-sufficient explanation; they are no more immune than is religious belief to the cross-pressures of fragilization, even though such modes seem to offer little or no conceptual space from which to affirm that humanity and the cosmos stand in relation to the divine reality Christian faith names as the God who both transcends the world and is immanently present to it.[33]

As Taylor notes, this fragilization impinges upon the immanent frame in a telling way with respect to the "buffered" identities the dynamics of secularity and its social imaginary have enabled us to construct. *All* of us now inhabit a human world in which many boundaries of meaning and practice that once delimited spaces for dwelling in secure possession of our identities—be they ethnic, linguistic, religious, or cultural—have increasingly become fragile and porous. Such fragilization makes possible an awareness of how deeply our identities are embedded in the otherness from which we delimit ourselves: The "other" already stands within the ambit of our identity to the extent that our identity and agency can be construed to be constituted in "immanent otherness." Fragilization thus provides a sharp and stark reminder that a fundamental human project is finding ways to dwell with one another, and to do so precisely in our mutual

32 Taylor, *A Secular Age*, 304. Even more telling would be framing the question as "Why *any* way at all?"

33 Taylor, *A Secular Age*, "The Immanent Frame," 539–93.

otherness. In the face of all the otherness we communally and individually both encounter and bring with us, it is no easy task to construct conditions for dwelling together in the contingencies of time upon the finite and fragile planet entrusted to us.

These are vulnerabilities that Neiman characterizes with the telling trope of "homeless," an image she uses to mark out a "metaphysic of permanent rupture" between the world as it is and the world as it ought to be: "The gap between nature and freedom, *is* and *ought*, conditions all human existence.... Integrity requires affirming the dissonance and conflict at the heart of experience. It means recognizing that we are never, metaphysically, at home in the world."[34] She sees this gap between "ought" and "is" driving our relentless human efforts to make sense of the world, even as modernity's disenchantment of the world has rendered the workings of nature void of meaning save in terms an efficient causality absent of purpose: "Are our capacities to find and create meaning in a world adequate to a world that seems determined to thwart them?"[35] This trope puts in stark terms the consequences of that disenchantment: "Despite its apparent modesty, home is too intentional a concept to be part of a disenchanted world. It's a metaphor that shows how much we lost when we lost the argument from design."[36] The sense that we are "homeless" is thus a sense that, at its deepest level, the world cares not to welcome us—because, it seems, the world *is such as not to care at all*. Viewed from the naturalist vantage the immanent frame provides, the world presents itself with a bleakness that is both poignant and intimidating.

Neiman's trope of homeless encompass a full range of human vulnerabilities, but it takes its most pronounced and intractable form as it arises in the face of those ravages of contingency we

---

34 Neiman, *Evil in Modern Thought*, 80.

35 Neiman, *Evil in Modern Thought*, 318; see also 322: "The drive to seek reason in the world—even, or especially, at the points where it seems most absent—is as deep a drive as any we have."

36 Neiman, *Evil in Modern Thought*, 304.

rightly name suffering and evil. She uses this trope to frame our human circumstances of a "conceptual helplessness" in the face of evil that seems to have taken intellectual hold in the aftermath of the massive horrors that humans have inflicted on one another since at least the start of the twentieth century—and continue to do so in the twenty-first. Yet her account of our being homeless is by no means devoid of hope, even in the face of the abyss of evil; the hope she holds out, in fact, is the quite robust hope she finds in a child's persistent quest to make sense of the world, a quest she sees marking our capacity to enact ways to make the world what it "ought to be" in our "homeless" human condition: a place in which we make one another welcome.

The space of hope that her account offers will thus help in delimiting one of the final contours for an anthropology of finite freedom that stands open to the workings of grace. Neiman's trope of "homeless" stands complementary to the trope of "hospitality" that Steiner uses to articulate the graced enactment that addresses the deep fractures of our "metaphysically homeless" human condition. Such enactment encompasses a full and reciprocal welcoming of one another's otherness that allows us even amid the fractures of secular times to dwell in mutuality as *both* guests and hosts to one another. This possibility arises in function of the recognition that *even though the world does not seem to welcome us, this in no way necessitates that we make one another unwelcome.* As Steiner quite aptly put it, "I believe we must teach other human beings to be guests of each other. . . . We must teach people we are guests of life on this crowded, polluted planet."[37]

I will then further—and finally—argue that a central component for a theological anthropology of situated freedom consists in our finite freedom's capacity to enact, in and through a hospitality fully attentive to our mutual human vulnerabilities, a "seeing good" that brings about the fullness of the very mutuality it sees as good. Such seeing and enacting good is one that is

37 George Steiner quoted in Theo Hobson, "On Being a Perfect Guest: The Tablet Interview: George Steiner," *The Tablet* 259 (August 13, 2005): 15.

informed by the graciousness of God's hospitality, a graciousness that Christian theology has articulated as a Triune enactment of good that may be discerned as the following:

- the seeing good that enacts creation as the space of otherness in which all that is contingent comes to be;
- the seeing good that enacts the Incarnation as the human enfleshment of the Word by which the divine transformatively takes into itself the brokenness of the world; and
- the seeing good that is pledged as eschatological completion, in and through the working of the Spirit in humanity and in the cosmos of which we are part, in the transformative outpouring of the Spirit from the crucified and risen Lord Jesus.

In consequence, our enactments of hospitality to one another, empowered by the divine seeing of good in its Triune inflections, become responses of our finite freedom that make it possible to turn even the fractured ground of the immanent frame of secularity into a place of graced and gracious welcome for the good of one another and of all that is other.[38]

---

38 For a thoughtful articulation of how a Trinitarian understanding of human relationality can be seen working within Taylor's anthropology, see Carlos D. Colorado, "Transcendent Sources and the Dispossession of the Self," in *Aspiring for Fullness in Secular Age*, 82–92. In the same volume Jennifer A. Herdt, in "The Authentic Individual in the Network of Agape," 191–92, notes a similar Trinitarian current: "We see fully for the first time [in *A Secular Age*] that Taylor's compelling appeal [to an expanding network of *agape*] is rooted not in a vague Romantic aestheticism, but in an endless love of the broken neighbor who stands 'among others in the stream of love which is that facet of God's life we try to grasp, very inadequately, in speaking of the trinity' [*A Secular Age*, 701]."

For an articulation of the way in which human finite freedom is rooted in the dynamics of the Trinity, see Philip J. Rossi, SJ, "Human Freedom and the Triune God," *T&T Clark Handbook of Theological Anthropology*, ed. Mary Ann Hinsdale and Stephen Oakey (New York: Bloomsbury, 2021), 123–34.

Chapter 2

Finitude, Contingency, and the Enclosed Horizons of Immanence

THE IMMANENT FRAME: NATURALISM AS SOCIAL IMAGINARY

THIS CHAPTER WILL EXAMINE THE fundamental challenge a culture of secularity presents to the articulation of a theological anthropology of situated human freedom that seeks to provide appropriate conceptual space from which to discern the enacted worldly presence of a transcendent God—namely, "grace"—at work even within the self-enclosed immanent frame of secularity. This challenge is both imaginative and conceptual. It arises in consequence of the reductive naturalism inscribed both into the characteristic social imaginary of secularity, "the immanent frame," and into the conceptual scaffolding that provides its argumentative support. The "immanent frame" circumscribes all value and meaning into naturalistic terms that are entirely "this-worldly": These terms provide no space for meaning, value, or reference other than what emerges from the constructive activities of human intelligence working within the confines of what is empirically accessible and measurable.[1]

---

1 "Empirically accessible," of course, admits of a range of construals, some of which allow "religious experience" to fall within the scope of accessibility. The construal I am offering here, particularly with respect to what I later term the most "stringent" naturalistic form of the immanent frame,

One consequence of this naturalistic circumscription has been to relegate religious modes of belief and practice, such as the monotheisms of the Abrahamic traditions, to the status of, at best, historically contingent cultural practices. On this account, such practices do not, as they often claim to do, serve to affirm as divine a reality that transcends the constructive capacities of human intelligence as it is ordered to and works upon what is empirically accessible. In the absence of any such cognitive import, such practices may be, at best, confined to the sphere of what is inwardly "private" or, at worst, based on illusions that need to be dispelled. In either case, the "faith" that is coordinate to and informs such practices is problematic. As private, it may be as much a source of personal dysfunction as of constructive stability; as illusory, it can and has become a kind of "social faith" that leads to divisiveness and destructive social conflict. Concomitant with this eclipse of transcendence, the discourse of grace as a marker of the transcendent God's engagement with the world, and the discourse of spirit as the animating principle relating humans to the transcendent, are most suitably consigned to dismissal into a realm of silence.

This chapter thus will probe, in a preliminary way, features of the social imaginary provided by the immanent frame for the conceptual and imaginative space they might nonetheless provide—despite this formidable naturalistic circumscription— for rendering a discourse of grace intelligible in two related ways. The first would be *within* the immanent frame—that is, in a way that engages its distinctive mode of making sense of the world in order to identify its limitations and the import of those limitations. The second would be *for* the immanent frame—that is, in a way that speaks to the human dynamisms structuring its ways of making sense, in order to articulate the pressures those dynamisms themselves place against the strictures

is one for which such claims fall outside what counts as empirically accessible. I have tried to indicate this restrictive construal by the additional
qualifier "measurable."

of the immanent frame. To do this requires at the outset a brief examination of, first, the strictures of closure that the immanent frame has placed upon the discourse of transcendence and grace and, second, the limits that these strictures also place on the capacity to speak adequately from within the immanent frame about the character of the human and its place in the cosmos.

As this examination unfolds, it will indicate how the connection between these two elements bears in a significant way upon the project of providing an anthropology of situated freedom that would make it possible to discern the workings of grace in a culture of secularity that structurally occludes their possibility. This connection will indicate how the limitations that are embedded in the immanent frame's capacity to speak adequately about the human indicate an ironic instability in the veto it places on the discourse of grace, spirit, and transcendence. Such instability functions to challenge and eventually undermine the closure that the naturalism of the immanent frame attempts to place upon questions of transcendence, grace, and the spiritual constitution of the human. The main locus of this instability, as the second section of this chapter proposes, can be found in the interplay among three elements that provide coordinates for the way in which the human condition is situated within the naturalistic frame of the secular social imaginary. The first is the contingency of the workings of a world in which things "go wrong" or counter to human plans and purposes. The second is the expectation that is then placed upon the instrumental use of reason to bend and control contingency to human purposes. The third is a self-understanding of human identity and agency that is constituted in abstraction from social relationality, a self-understanding that Taylor calls "the buffered self." The interplay of these elements—particularly the pressures they put upon, first, the adequacy of the buffered self to serve as an account of human identity and agency as it is situated in the workings of contingency and, second, upon the capacity of the naturalist veto to preclude in toto the discourses of transcendence, spirit, and grace—will help to point out possibilities for discerning the workings of grace within and upon the fractures that pressure the self-sufficiency of the immanent frame.

THE NATURALIST VETO

There are a variety of ways to construe the origin and the functioning of the naturalist veto upon anything other than inner-worldly explication and validation of our human modes of engagement with the world and with one another. One way is in terms of the processes of "disenchantment," often seen as characteristic of modernity, through which the language and forms of scientific inquiry and conceptualization displaced modes of explanation that appealed to forces or agency working upon or within the things of the world from a sphere of reality that is different from the empirically accessible. A second, related way of construing the naturalist veto is in terms of the erosion and loss of any semantics of intrinsic meaning that index the nature, operation, and place of things of the world to the finalities that give the world its order. The naturalism of the immanent frame stands far removed from the naturalism of an Aristotelian world in which a "nature" may be correctly and aptly described in terms of the finality that expresses the principle giving order to something's activity. It is, instead, a naturalism of merely efficient causality for which finality, save for some residual usefulness it may have as a shorthand for ends and purposes that agents adopt with intent, has become otiose for the language of explanation.[2]

On either construal, to the extent that modernity's social imaginary remains deeply etched into our bearing toward the workings of the world, we now live and act as part of a world

2 George Steiner has cogently expressed the importance that this latter construal of the natural has had for the formative dynamics of modernity: "*It is this break of the covenant [of meaning] between word and world which constitutes one of the very few genuine revolutions of spirit in Western history, and which defines modernity itself.*" *Real Presences* (Chicago: University of Chicago Press, 1989), 93, emphasis in original.

in which "nature" has been fully disenchanted of any purposes that might be thought to pay attention to humanity and its aims and purposes. Even more ominously, we live and act in a world in which we have become acutely aware of how thoroughly we have become agents of disenchantment and of disengagement of ourselves from attention to the humanity of others and, indeed, to our own humanity. As Susan Neiman has noted, in a world in which scientific inquiries have disenchanted us from seeing the operation of supernatural agencies, the distinction between natural evil, such as earthquakes, and moral evil, wrought by the hands and intentions of human agents, can no longer function as the trusted conceptual tool to divide human moral responsibility for evil from the human misfortune that ensues in consequence of floods, storms, and earthquakes: "Science may have abolished the sense that the world is inhabited by forces with wills of their own, and in this way reduced the *unheimlich*. But the price is enormous, for all nature stands condemned. Human beings themselves become walking indictments of creation."[3] On either construal, moreover, the immanent frame—particularly at its most stringently naturalistic—thus provides little conceptual, grammatical, or imaginative space for articulating a discourse of the divine, a discourse of the spiritual, or a discourse of grace. It precludes affirming the divine as a transcendent actuality, speaking of the spiritual as a constitutive element of our own human identity, or articulating discourse about an order of grace in "excess" of the natural, an order that expresses the enacted worldly presence of that transcendent God and the bearing of that presence upon our human condition.

This naturalist veto suggests that the operative assumptions of the self-enclosed explanatory dynamics of the immanent frame present quite formidable challenges to the articulation of what it seems to preclude: an anthropology of situated freedom indexed to the task of rendering intelligible the discourses of grace,

3 Susan Neiman, *Evil in Modern Thought: An Alternative History of Philosophy* (Princeton: Princeton University Press, 2002), 236–37.

transcendence, and spirit. There is, moreover, a further challenge the immanent frame poses that may be even more fundamental. These operative naturalistic assumptions challenge the very intelligibility of the project of articulating an anthropology of "situated freedom," inasmuch as such a project requires careful attention to the dynamics and modalities of human self-understanding that enable humanity to locate itself within the workings of nature and culture. What makes this project problematic from the perspective of the immanent frame is that its own reductive explanatory dynamics provide little room for the self-interpretation that orients such an anthropological project and provides coordinates for articulating the specific modalities and contexts in which human freedom finds itself situated.[4] From the perspective of the immanent frame, any anthropology indexed to the questions about what it is to be human that arise within and from human reflective self-understanding will eventually find itself outside the parameters of the empirically descriptive and measurable that constitute its conditions for genuine cognition.

One reason why this further challenge is important is that it points to a connection that is at least implicit in the naturalist veto with respect to the transcendent: How we view what it is to be human, in an important sense, is *already* in function of what we take to be the possibility—or the impossibility—of affirming that the human may stand in actual relation to the transcendent. Put

4 This point could be put more sharply: it is at least arguable that the kind of naturalist presuppositions that have shaped the immanent frame eventually render unintelligible any account of human freedom that is indexed to human self-understanding. (Kant makes a parallel point in the *Critique of Practical Reason* [KprV AA 5:97/Cam 218] when he remarks that if freedom were construed from a perspective in which the only causality deemed intelligible is the efficient causality of nature represented empirically, then human freedom "would at bottom be nothing better than the freedom of a turnspit.") Even more sharply, these naturalist presuppositions may make it unintelligible—or otiose—to ask: What does it mean to be human? Taylor has explicitly described his body of work as a sustained effort to show the incoherence of reductive naturalisms with regard to their understanding of the human inasmuch as they are unable to account for the self-interpreting activity that is fundamental in constituting what it is to be human.

more directly, our understanding of the anthropological, what it is to be human, *already implicates the theological*, our understanding of what it is to be godly; and our understanding of the theological conversely implicates the anthropological. There is no indifferent or innocent neutrality about the human here. It is at peril to its own principles for naturalism to leave a space in its account of what it is be human from which there is a genuine possibility of truly standing in relation to the transcendent; and it is at a similar peril to its own principles for a theological anthropology to close off any dimension of the human or of the cosmos it understands to be God's creation to the possibility of being, however unlikely it may seem, a locus for the working of grace.

What this suggests with respect to the immanent frame is that we may be more likely to identify an appropriate locus from which to render a discourse of grace intelligible to a culture of secularity in terms of what it says—or says by implication, or even does not say—about the human than in terms of what it says—or does not say—about God. Conversely, in articulating an anthropology of grace, it will be important to be attentive to what it says, or does not say, about God, as an important locus for what it implies about how the human is to be understood. It is thus a matter of no little import to articulate the parameters the immanent frame sets for how we may construe what it is to be human, since that may also bring to light important features of its veto upon discourse about God and of the basis for that veto that otherwise might remain unnoticed and implicit. As will be noted later, one of these features seems to be a presumption that human freedom cannot but stand in rivalry—indeed, in zero-sum competition—with God's freedom; and in this it mirrors the zero-sum dynamic embedded in the exercise of human freedom. This presumption, I will be arguing later, stands in opposition to an understanding of the manner in which the "original grace" of creation provides space for the exercise of human freedom, not as space of emulation and rivalry, but as a fundamental mode both of human mutual relationality and of human relationality to God.

There can be little doubt that the cultures of secularity have said and continue to say much about what it is to be human, but what has been put forth cannot yet be considered to constitute a consensus, let alone a single coherent anthropology. Of at least equal, if not greater, import may be what these cultures have not directly said about the human, but have rather left implicit as elements of the larger framework within which the immanent frame explicates the world in the natural, social, and cultural dimensions in which the human is situated. The work that Taylor, Neiman, and Steiner, among others, have done in examining the way in which modernity and its secular aftermath understand both the human and the world in which it is situated, has, however, served to identify key aspects of what has been left implicit and unarticulated.[5] The identification they provide of these implicit elements will be of value for my efforts to articulate an anthropology of situated freedom that offers a way to render grace intelligible within the very contexts upon which the naturalist veto seems to have a firm hold. Each of them has been especially astute in bringing to light, in different ways, some of the morally normative presuppositions that are just as important as naturalistic ones for orienting the construal that the social imaginary of the immanent frame gives to the human and the human condition. Taylor does so in terms of his excavation of the moral sources motivating modernity's construction of "the buffered self." Neiman does so in terms of bringing the concern with the problem of evil to center stage in the story of the emergence of modern philosophy. And Steiner does so in terms of discerning, at the core of the modern concern about the loss of meaning, a theological struggle over whether humanity can now rightly claim to have displaced God as the authentic agent of creation. Their work provides useful guidance, first, for articulating key elements

5 One element of the argument of *Sources of the Self* consists of bringing the cultures of modernity to account with regard to their "inarticulacy" about the nature and the role of their "moral sources." Charles Taylor, *Sources of the Self: The Making of the Modern Identity* (Cambridge, MA: Harvard University Press, 1989), 91–107.

implicit in the larger framework for situating the human that bear upon secularity's understanding of the human and, second, for acutely discerning the tensions in which these elements stand in relation to one another.

One illustration of the interplay between what is said and what is left implicit about the human can be seen by considering just one instance of the ambiguous role that a notion of "progress" has had as the social imaginary of the immanent frame has taken shape in the emergence of secular modernity. At an earlier point in the emergence of cultures of secularity, it may have appeared that there had developed a broad consensus, especially among thinkers considered representative of "The Enlightenment," that humanity was fixed upon a general course of historical progress, yet a closer examination of their texts paints a different, more ambivalent picture. Not only was there significant variance about the character of such progress among those who affirmed such an upward trajectory, but there was also a similarly varied range of important dissenting views, including those held by figures favorably disposed to other tenets typically associated with the Enlightenment. In addition, whether the dynamism of progress was something that could be considered a constitutive element of the human, or was rather the outcome of elements in the larger context in which humanity found itself—or even something that was subject to reversal—was a matter of dispute. In consequence, even a number of those, such as Kant, who can ultimately be counted among those who give a qualified endorsement to human progress struggled to make that endorsement conceptually coherent in view of considerations about the character of the human and the conditions in which humanity is situated that heavily weigh against it.[6]

6 Important loci for the development of Kant's views on this point are his various discussions of "cosmopolitanism" and the moral and natural dynamics by which a world order conductive to "perpetual peace" can be brought about. Of note for later purposes in my argument is that one mark of this struggle is that Kant considers it important to draw a distinction between "optimism" about human moral progress and "hope" for human

As Neiman's compelling study *Evil in Modern Thought* indicates, it was not only with respect to the notion of progress that Kant showed an acute awareness of the important bearing that our understanding of the world in which humanity is situated has upon our understanding of our own humanity. For Kant, such awareness of the character of the world in which humanity is situated is of utmost importance for understanding an element that is at the very core of his critical philosophy: We are properly constituted as human in the exercise of the finite freedom of our embodied human agency. As a result, articulating an understanding of the specific elements that constitute the situated character of human freedom—that it is the exercise of a finite reason embodied in space and time in a world of nature operating in accord with causal principles for which space and time are conditions of possibility—thus provides a fundamental frame of reference for Kant's understanding of the constitutive role that the freedom of human agency plays in what it is to be human. The spatio-temporal world in which human freedom is situated is one in which moral intelligibility is framed not merely in terms of an ordering in accord with the theoretical use of human reason that explicates the workings of nature. It is, rather, a world to which the responsible exercise of human freedom *must bring reason's demand for moral intelligibility and take responsibility for enacting that demand.* It is in bringing the demand for moral intelligibility to the world and taking responsibility for enacting it in the world—in Kant's terms, in heeding the demand of the categorical imperative by enacting it—that we orient our own self-understanding of what it is to be human to the moral exercise of our finite freedom that is a core constitutive element of our humanity.

Neiman's discussion of Kant's attentiveness to the importance of the conditions within which humanity is situated for

moral progress. He does not endorse the former, but he does consider the latter not only to have a basis in the exercise of practical reason but to have an important function in sustaining human moral effort to bring these social ideals to actuality.

articulating what it is to be human thus provides a lesson for the purposes of making explicit how the social imaginary of the immanent frame understands what it is to be human within the context of secularity. The lesson is this: In order to see, engage, and evaluate the full picture of how the human is construed from within the perspective of the immanent frame, it will be necessary to articulate what this naturalistic frame of reference also takes to be the circumstances and conditions of our human situatedness in the plural, global, and increasingly interdependent culture of the twenty-first century. As the next section will indicate, there is good reason to think that the account that the immanent frame, under the naturalist veto, can provide of the circumstances and conditions of fractured and contested meaning in which humanity is now located stands, ironically, in deep tension with what, under the same veto, it permits us to construe as constitutive of what it is to be human. We find ourselves in circumstances that require us to enact the very self-understanding of our humanity for which a naturalist construal of the human from the immanent frame provides little or no space.

FRACTURED HORIZONS AND THE FRAGMENTED SPACES OF CONTINGENCY

There are thus a number of reasons why it is important to attend to the ways in which the immanent frame, as the social imaginary of secularity, construes the conditions in which humanity is situated. The most general of these reasons is the one already noted as exemplified in Neiman's discussion of Kant: Providing the larger picture in which an account of the human is placed makes it possible to discern and articulate important features of that account that otherwise might remain only implicit. In the case of the immanent frame, I will thus first look at a set of historical and sociocultural dynamics that Taylor, Neiman, and Steiner have identified as increasingly characteristic of the pluralized and interdependent world in which we find ourselves situated in the early twenty-first century. I will then examine the role these dynamics play in the accounts that the immanent frame can provide of the shape and significance of our human condition. Next I will argue that the elements that bear closest attention in these accounts are those that display, in a variety of ways, the deep fractures and the incompletions that humans experience in engaging the world—or, as Neiman quite directly puts it, "the fact that *things go wrong*."[7] This sense that "things go wrong" seems to have intensified throughout the range of humanity experience, most notably in terms of our relations to one another, our relations to the natural and social worlds in which we dwell, and our efforts then to render intelligible our human place in what presents itself as a world of all too often unreliable and uncertain outcome.

I will then propose that this sense of fracture, which manifests the thoroughness of the contingency of our human circumstances, stands as an important point of reference to two other points of coordination for situating what it is to be human in the cultures of secularity for which the immanent frame is the operative social imaginary. One of these coordinates is the central place that has been given within the circumstances of fracture to the project of exercising human control over the workings of contingency. Within this coordinate, the instrumentalization of reason looms large as the manner in which humanity can empower itself to bring about the diminution, if not the elimination, of "things going wrong." A further coordinate will then be provided by an important shift that has taken place with respect to the role that social relationality places in the constitution of our human identity. This shift is from a social embedding of the self, in which a central factor in articulating one's identity was one's place in a multilevel set of interlocking social relations, to forms of autonomous agency in which one's individually formed identity stands prior to fundamental societal relations, in which one stands as a contracting party on equal status with all other contracting

7 Neiman, *Evil in Modern Thought*, 81, emphasis in original.

parties. After an overview of some of the salient features of each of these coordinates, I will then examine how they function to provide an account of our human circumstances and condition that, despite its apparent closure to taking these as vectors orienting us to a more fundamental coordinate of relationality—namely, to a relationality oriented to divine transcendence—still bears within itself dynamisms that have intelligibility only by reference to such relationality.

My argument here, however, will not be that widespread fracture and its coordinate elements represent something entirely new that entered into the human condition in the wake of secularity. It will be, rather, that modernity and the secularity that is its offspring have made it possible to discern in new and challenging ways the depth and the extent of that fracture, not only in the conditions in which we are situated, but also in our very makeup as human and the possibilities we envision for our human future as part of the place in the cosmos with which we have been entrusted. One provocative way to express this challenge is that the secularity, which has made manifest a distinctively modern cognizance of the deeply historical character of the fractured circumstances of the human world, has also drawn attention to the equally deep fractures in what constitutes us "all the way down" (i.e., metaphysically) as human. I will then further argue that, even as the immanent frame has helped us to recognize the depth and extent of such fracture as a historically formative element of the human condition, it has not yet taken sufficient cognizance of the ways in which recognition of the depth of this fracture also puts in question its naturalistically framed understanding of what it is to be human.

Recognition of the depth of this fracture, moreover, has major bearing upon how it now stands in relation to two other points of reference crucial for the structure and working of the immanent frame: first, the possibilities it provides for human control over "things going wrong" and, second, the adequacy of its account of our identity and agency as disembedded from social relationality. One result, then, of putting Neiman's lesson to work here is that it offers a way to identify and to articulate important tensions in the way the immanent frame understands what it is to be human. These tensions encompass questions of whether and how the circumstances of the deep fracture of the human world, manifest as the contingency of its history, also manifest a contingency that is "metaphysical," one that goes "all the way down" into the constitution of what it is to be human. These questions bear upon the interplay among the worldly contingency of "things gone wrong," human efforts to overcome contingency though instrumental reason, and our understanding of ourselves as autonomous agents exercising freedom in the moral space constituted by the cosmos and by our relations to one another. I will be arguing that it is in this interplay that space may open up for discerning the presence and the operation of grace, particularly as a function of attending to the coordinates that constitute the relational moral space in which we exercise our human freedom.

Showing those tensions in the immanent frame, however, is hardly enough by itself to demonstrate that a more adequate account of the human and of the circumstances in which it is situated is thereby given by an account that then discerns the human in relation to transcendence.[8] More than a single line of critical argument countering the implicit anthropology of the immanent frame is needed to make a positive case on behalf of an anthropology of situated freedom that takes the intelligibility of that freedom to be embedded in a relationship that is graced by its receptivity to a transcendent God. I will thus be constructing this account, at least in part, as offering a challenge to the account of the human implicit in the immanent frame on a ground that it claims for its own and also claims as one of the strongest bases for

8 It may be the case that there are ways in which this tension may be resolved by maintaining some version of the naturalist veto. I will suggest later that, first, the kind of neo-Lucretian view articulated in the work of David Hume may provide a plausible way to do so and, second, that this represents the far more challenging modality of closing the immanent frame to transcendence by its practical shrug of indifference than the closure offered in the arguments of theoretical atheists, be they old or "new."

its invocation of the naturalistic veto—namely, the fractured and fragmented circumstances in which humanity has now come to find itself situated and that, when read in a naturalistic register, are seen as clearly and unarguably indicative that all attempts to "prove" the existence of God and, even more so, to construct a theodicy are futile: There is not, never was, and never will be an all-powerful, all knowing, and all loving God.[9] I will propose, instead, that orienting an account of the human to the fractured horizons and the fragmented landscape of the human condition that the immanent frame has helped us even more fully discern may, in fact, prove quite central for constructing a theology of grace properly attentive to the circumstances in which the exercise of human freedom—which is fundamental to the modality of our human response to grace—is now increasingly immersed.

This leads to a further, more constructive reason that will be operative in the second part of my discussion of how the immanent frame construes the conditions in which humanity is situated. I will be arguing that the immanent frame of secularity, in drawing attention to the fragile and deeply fractured dynamics at work within both humanity's quest to make sense of the world and the contexts out of which humanity seeks to find that sense, has provided important conceptual and imaginative resources for an anthropology of situated freedom. These are resources that help efforts to understand and to articulate the multiple and incomplete character of the human receptivity into which God seeks entry in grace and for which grace must itself have an appropriate operative modality.

This claim, of course, goes counter (and intentionally so) to the assumption that the self-enclosed explanatory dynamics of

9 It is important to note that the counter-position I am offering will not dispute the futility of the theodicy that has been a staple of modern discussions; it disputes, instead, the presumption that such failure necessarily entails a denial of a transcendent God. In fact, it even suggests that "the failure of theodicy" may itself be requisite—as it was in the case of Job—as a pointer to a more adequate understanding (or a less inadequate misunderstanding!) of what constitutes God's transcendence.

the immanent frame often make about its closure to transcendence. This is the assumption that the fractured circumstances in which humanity is situated, and about which modernity has left no doubt regarding their import, count unquestionably and decisively against the workings of grace—or of anything "in" or "of" the world—as indicative of a transcendent presence to which our humanity is ordered. Against this I will be proposing that taking such fracture to be a crucial locus in which grace may be discerned provides a way to see in one of secularity's notable manifestations of fragmentation—what Taylor calls the "nova effect" of a multiplicity of contested options for belief and unbelief that "fragilizes" all belief (including its own unbelief)—something other than a confusing darkness that bespeaks an absence of grace. Taking such fracture as a key locus for discerning grace will make it possible to see it instead as drawing attention to the richly varied tinder of the human spirit that is being ignited by God's spirit into patterns of light and warmth, manifesting the reach of God's love, which we had only barely glimpsed before.

My argument has already indicated a number of times that, in a world of disenchanted secularity in which the natural world runs its course indifferent to human purposes and humanity's own complicity in the divisions and violence that seem incessantly to tear at the fabric of society, the fracture that ensues from each of these vectors needs to be ingredient in the immanent frame's depiction of the human condition. From the perspective of the immanent frame, however, it is unclear whether it makes any difference morally to distinguish between the fracture that runs through the conditions in which humanity is situated and the one that places humans in conflict with one another. Neiman's reading of the history of modern philosophy and the intellectual culture of which it is a part suggests that a thoroughly consistent naturalism could not but conclude to the persistent inevitability of fracture in both cases. Such a conclusion seems even more compelling when placed against what she takes to be the limitations on human capacity to exercise full control over the workings of nature, as well as over ourselves as part of that nature. On Neiman's reading of intellectual history, Nietzsche and Freud provide the final arguments for a relentless naturalism that reveals how stripped of all comfort the disenchanted world must be. She writes, "It would be easy to acknowledge that not controlling the world is part of being human, were it not for the fact that *things go wrong*. The thought that the rift between reason and nature is neither error nor punishment but the fault line along which the universe is structured can be a source of perfect terror."[10] Neiman's account, with good reason, puts into question whether a sharp distinction can be made—at least with respect to our understanding of humanity and of the fractured condition in which humanity dwells—between the "metaphysical" and the "historical." The historicizing of human reason that was one important outcome of nineteenth-century philosophy need not, as one influential version of the emergence of secularity would have it, result in the abolition of metaphysics; it might, instead, require us to recognize history as itself ingredient in the constitutive metaphysical makeup of what it is to be human.

The question of the mutual bearing that history and metaphysics have to each other is undoubtedly implicated in the articulation of an anthropology of situated freedom and an assessment of the adequacy of the construal of what it is to be human provided by the immanent frame. While even successfully accomplishing both of these particular tasks will not be sufficient for settling this larger issue, setting out the terms of the tension at work in the immanent frame's construal of our human situatedness, and then using that to assess its account of the human, will itself nonetheless help in exhibiting key elements of the issues at stake. An appropriate place to start will be by taking fracture and fragmentation—or to recall Neiman's phrase, the fact that "things go wrong"—to be, in the first instance, fully historical phenomena that manifest themselves at particular times and places, affecting

10 Neiman, *Evil in Modern Thought*, 80–81.

particular individuals, communities, and cultures. Some fracture and fragmentation is small and of little consequence—an item misplaced, an appointment missed, a stumble that leads to a minor bruise—while some is large and of much greater consequence—a tornado, an economic crisis, a civil war—disrupting the lives and plans of many.

Within the perspective provided by the immanent frame, moreover, the fracture and fragmentation, be it large or small, occasioned by things gone wrong takes place within the coordinates of a disenchanted history, one in which there never was an innocent "once upon a time" in which everything in life fit together all the time for everyone. A disenchanted history is one that moves willy-nilly, neither guided from without by providence, nor impelled along a trajectory of immanent teleology from within, nor drawn out into an inexorable preordered unfolding that the tropes of fate, predestination, and the dialectic of history have variously expressed. A disenchanted history is one that is thoroughly imbued with the workings of a contingency of uncertain outcome that arises from the complex interplay of the variety of agencies and forces that constitute the concrete, embodied, finite human condition, most notably human decision and interaction as they are shaped in a variety of sociocultural matrices, and the processes and the limitations of a natural world that constitutes the physical environment for the planetary life of which the human species is a part.

This interplay of the forces of contingency that lead to the uncertain outcomes of the things that go wrong by thwarting human plans, purposes, or desires is not, however, totally arbitrary or capricious. In fact, the forces in play include those of the environing world whose workings the natural sciences emergent with modernity have articulated with increasing theoretical acumen and detail. Even as these theoretical accounts have shifted from modes of predictability that are represented as fully deterministic (in the manner of Newtonian physics) to ones governed by statistical patterns of probability, the ideal of minimizing uncertainty with regard to the outcome that results when these forces are in play has remained constant. As many accounts of the development of modernity have noted, this ideal of maximizing the predictability of the workings of nature has been concomitant with a counterpart ideal that reconfigures the human relation to nature. A relation that had previously been understood in terms of seeking to know and to act in accord with humanity's proper place in a well-fixed order of nature is now reconstructed, if not replaced, by an ideal of acting to maximize the range of human direction and control over the workings of nature. One result has been what many of these accounts see as the rise of "instrumental reason," which functions as the crucial modality for the exercise of human control of the forces at play in the workings of the world's contingency. The power of human control that resides in the instrumental use of reason now serves as the basis for an expectation that, on the basis of this capacity, humanity can make progress in endeavors to reduce the likelihood that the workings of contingency will result in things going wrong.[11] The taming of contingency by the control that instrumental reason makes possible stands as a key set of coordinates for situating the human in terms of the immanent frame.

Taylor has noted that, in the dynamics that shaped the immanent frame into the social imaginary of modernity, the central role given to instrumental reason for bringing nature under human control has been concomitant with a shift in human self-understanding from the "porous self" of the premodern "enchanted" world to the "disengaged" or "buffered" self of disenchanted secularity. He elaborates on the constitutive features of such self-understanding by noting that—despite the fact that language, which he terms "the web of interlocution" to designate the social embedding of language, provides what he considers the

11 It is becoming increasingly evident that what might be called "lived counter-arguments" against a presumed upward trajectory of benefit in consequence of human efforts at instrumental control of nature are becoming powerfully emergent as our human activities move the planet closer to a number of "tipping points" for both local and widespread environmental disaster.

necessary matrix for human self-understanding—the "punctual self" is a self-construal that is, in contrast, "monological."[12] He writes, "Modern culture has developed conceptions of individualism which picture the human person as, at least potentially, finding his or her own bearings within, declaring independence from the web of interlocution which have originally formed him/her, or at least neutralizing them."[13] In linking the development of a self-understanding that construes the core of human identity in monological terms with the placement of instrumental reason at the center of humanity's relation to nature, Taylor provides a further coordinate to "contingency" and "control" for marking out the perspective from which the immanent frame construes the elements that constitute our situated human condition. Along this coordinate, the framing of the core of our individual human identity is disembedded from any constitutive social relationship. While this "disembedding" has historically played itself out in variety of ways, including forms of radical individualism, a powerful trope signaling that the individual stands constitutively prior to any form of (public) social relationship has been "the social contract." Though the punctual self is presumed to stand as originally disembedded from any constitutive social relationality, its constitution and operation as atomistic is fraught with consequences for the construal and functioning of any relationality into which it then enters.

In many of the standard narratives of Western philosophy, the Cartesian *cogito*, particularly when it is taken to function in an environment prepared by late medieval nominalism, performed the first major uprooting of the understanding of the

12 "My self definition is understood as an answer to the question Who am I. And this question finds its original sense in the interchange of speakers. I define who I am by defining where I speak from, in the family tree, in social space, in the geography of social statuses and functions, in my intimate relations to the ones I love.... This obviously cannot be a contingent matter. There is no way we could be inducted into personhood except by being initiated into a language" (Taylor, *Sources of the Self*, 35).

13 Taylor, *Sources of the Self*, 36.

self from its linguistic and social relationality. Taylor's work, however, by reminding us of the deeper Augustinian roots of the turn to self-reflexivity, indicates that there continue to be other possibilities—the most fruitful of which lie along paths that recover a sense of social relationality—for reenacting in and for a time of secularity the turn to the subject that allow a renewed and robust self-understanding of our identity as socially constituted. One of these possibilities for a renewed self-understanding of the social constitution of our identity arises in what he terms "languages of personal resonance," particularly when they are placed in the context of the self-decentering encounters with the world that he designates as the "epiphanic"—that is, "a manifestation which brings us into the presence of something which is otherwise inaccessible . . . which also defines or completes something, even as it reveals."[14] A second possibility for such a renewed self-understanding, which is not expressly considered by Taylor, focuses on dislodging the autonomy of human moral freedom from its long-presumed home in the dynamics of social atomism and resituating it as embedded in a mutual recognition of agency that takes form in practices of mutual social acknowledgment and respect. Both of these possibilities enable the self *to locate its identity in a space of otherness.* As I will argue in detail later, each of these possibilities for socially locating human identity is of import for the articulation of an anthropology of a situated freedom that is called upon in this time of secularity to participate in enacting grace in the spaces of otherness.

The first possibility is of import in that the languages of personal resonance and the epiphanic both function within what Taylor sees as a distinctively modern sense of expressive "inner depth," which has been a key element in the immanent frame's construal of what it is to be human. At the same time, in view of both their function and history, which are connected with the retrieval of an expressivist account of language, they are open to being construed as providing humans with a crucial mode

14 Taylor, *Sources of the Self*, 419.

of active participation in the grace constituted by the "seeing good" of God that is operative in creation and in the Incarnation. Taylor writes, "Put in yet other terms, the world's being good may now be seen as not entirely independent of our seeing it and showing it as good, at least as far as the world of humans is concerned."[15]

The second possibility, the social reembedding of human autonomy as a condition for its intelligibility and exercise, is in its turn of particular import in that this account of autonomy does not—as accounts of the human condition rendered from the perspective of the immanent frame tend to do—inevitably set humanity as a whole, nor set individual human agents, in a zero-sum agential competition with one another and, often enough, with a transcendent God. It thus provides some of the conceptual space needed to see the operation of grace as deeply embedded in social relationality both as it constitutes our humanity and as it stands as a graced orientation of humanity to the transcendent actuality of God.

What has been provided so far is only a sketchy outline of three important coordinates—contingency, control, and autonomy—from which to locate important features of the human condition from the perspective of the characteristic social imaginary of the cultures of secularity, the immanent frame. This outline so far has suggested some of the important modes of their interplay and has expressed hope that that interplay has some potentiality for opening up spaces from which the discourses of grace, transcendence, and spirit may be rendered intelligible for a culture of secularity. There is much detail, however, that needs to be filled in to make a robust case that these coordinates play the role that my argument claims they do and that their interplay opens up a direction along which speaking of grace can begin to make sense in a world of deep human fracture.

The next chapter will thus take up the work of filling in the detail with respect to the human condition as envisioned from the

15 Taylor, *Sources of the Self*, 448.

immanent frame and the tension in which its naturalist construal of that condition stands to the reflective dynamisms at work in human self-understanding. Of primary import here will be the horizon of hope that orients human efforts to render the workings of contingency morally intelligible. That inner tension will point toward possibilities for enlarging the horizon of the immanent frame by a multidimensional reorienting of efforts to make sense of our human place in the fractured spaces of contingency, particularly by empowering enactments of welcoming and accompaniment. The subsequent chapters will take up in turn three of the major reorientations involved in opening up such possibilities. The first involves reorienting the interplay of fracture and control in a world of contingency so that it is inflected not simply in terms of its adventitious impingement upon human vulnerability but also in terms of the radical dependence that constitutes the world as created; the second involves the engagement of a socially resituated autonomy with the dynamics of human fracture; the third consists of articulating the contours of a transformative self-involving "seeing good" that opens the "epiphanic" as locus of grace in a fractured world.

Part II

Contingency and the Persistence of Grace

Chapter 3

Charting the Landscape of Fracture

The fact that the world contains neither justice nor meaning threatens our ability both to act in the world and to understand it.

—Susan Neiman, *Evil in Modern Thought*

The modern world shows itself at once powerful and weak, capable of the noblest deeds or the foulest; before it lies the path to freedom or to slavery, to progress or retreat, to brotherhood or hatred. Moreover, man is becoming aware that it is his responsibility to guide aright the forces which he has unleashed and which can enslave him or minister to him. That is why he is putting questions to himself.

—Vatican Council II, *Gaudium et Spes*

PREMONITIONS AND PRECURSORS: SEEING THE SHADOWS WITHIN AN AGE OF ENLIGHTENMENT

AMONG THE CRUCIAL ELEMENTS SHAPING the immanent frame as the social imaginary of secularity were powerful intellectual currents that, even as they wrought the displacement of humanity from the center of the physical cosmos, enabled humanity to begin to order the world to serve human purposes, often in ways that had previously seemed unimaginable. In enlarging the reach of human technological control over processes of the physical universe, the use of instrumental reason altered human understanding of nature from a realm whose workings required acquiescence to its all too often hidden purposes into a field over which the increasing reach of human measurable and measuring knowledge promised proportionate ability to direct its working to serve human intents and desires. There is, however, something significantly more at stake in this altering of our understanding of humanity's relation to nature: as Louis Dupré has argued, in changing what we understand nature to be and thereby how we take ourselves to stand in relation to nature, we also bring about a change in nature itself.[1] Implicit in Dupré's argument is that, to the extent that we understand ourselves to be part of that nature, we are also changed by this shift in our understanding—dramatically so, since we seem to have enlarged considerably the scope of the use of instrumental reason to direct and control ourselves and the circumstances of our human lives. History and culture are fraught with metaphysical implications and, as this and the subsequent chapters will propose, those implications provide the horizon from which to open possibilities for the discernment of grace upon the fractured terrain of secular culture.

In this chapter I will chart two important dynamics at work within this change. They each have a bearing upon the ways in which the deeply fractured condition of humanity is implicated in the social imaginary of the immanent frame. The first dynamic is one that Susan Neiman has charted as a major current in the intellectual culture of modernity: the intractable challenge that evil in its full array of manifestations presents to the human drive to render all things intelligible, the drive she sees at the core of what has been termed the principle of "sufficient reason." She finds the lineaments of this dynamic in the work of key figures in

1 Most extensively in Louis Dupré, *Passage to Modernity: An Essay in the Hermeneutics of Nature and Culture* (New Haven, CT: Yale University Press, 1993).

the history of modern and contemporary philosophy, a number of whom were quite prescient with respect to later modernity in their diagnosis of the depth of the fracture that runs through the human condition. She thus recenters the history of modern philosophy from a focus upon the epistemic concerns represented by the Cartesian *cogito* to one that points to evil as the rift in moral intelligibility that delimits the nature and scope of the challenge of making human sense of a disenchanted world.

Taking note of her account is important for constructing an anthropology of situated freedom in the cultures of secularity for two reasons. First, it sees the attentiveness that late modernity has increasingly paid to the condition of fracture as a function, at least in part, of the trajectory of modern philosophy as it articulates more fully the implications that the disenchantment of the world has for our self-understanding of what it is to be human. Her account thus provides a path for discerning the process in which the change Dupré has noted has taken place; it offers a way to see how the construal that the immanent frame presents of the disenchanted world in which we are situated is deeply intertwined with the construal it coordinately presents of what it is to be human in such a world. Second, it is an account that recognizes that there is no neutrality with respect to the theological implications of how we construe what it is to be human and the circumstances that situate us in our efforts to live in consonance with that construal. What we take the human to be implicates what we take the transcendent to be—*even including taking it to be impossible*. Although in *Evil in Modern Thought* Neiman remains circumspect about her own theological views, she leaves little doubt that the questions about how the human stands in relationship to transcendence and how that transcendent may be construed *both* need to be engaged in any account we give of what it is to be human and of our human circumstances.

The second dynamic at work in this change of our human way of understanding and relating to nature is the play of contingency within the human condition in and through which fracture becomes concretely manifest. Within the course of my discussion I will be proposing that the fracture within the human condition upon which the immanent frame has focused our attention has primarily been located in terms of one of two important inflections of contingency—that is, differences in the manner in which a relation may be construed as contingent. This first inflection, which will be termed the "contingency of uncertain outcome," contains the dynamics by which "things go wrong" in the workings of the world that constitutes our human circumstances. The demand for moral intelligibility arises within the workings of this inflection of contingency, and it is this demand—which Neiman articulates as a demand for the world to be as "it ought to be"—that manifests the tension between the construal the immanent frame enables us to give, on the one hand, of what it is to be human and, on the other, of the world in which our humanity is situated. The second inflection of contingency, which will be the focus of the next chapter, will be termed the "contingency of radical dependence," a contingency whose working and intelligibility is conceptually and historically indexed to the articulation of the doctrine of creation forged in the matrix of the theological traditions of the Abrahamic religions. This inflection of contingency marks the radical dependence within which the cosmos stands—that is, it is *not* self-originating—as well as the gracious free abundance out of which it is both brought to be and sustained. As I will be arguing in the course of subsequent chapters, it is within the first inflection of contingency that, in both ordinary and in surprising ways, we find ourselves invited to participate in the enactment of grace; it is attention to the second inflection of contingency, however, that makes *it possible to discern as invitations to grace* the very workings of the fractured reality of our human makeup and the fractured circumstances of our human condition. As a result, attention to both inflections of contingency will be fundamental for articulating an anthropology of situated freedom that opens space for discerning grace in a time of secularity.

EVIL AND THE IMMANENT FRAME

Neiman's *Evil in Modern Thought: An Alternative History of Philosophy* makes a provocative case for two theses that are particularly helpful for seeing how the deeply fractured condition of humanity is implicated in the social imaginary of the immanent frame. The first thesis is a claim about the fundamental intellectual trajectory of modernity that disputes the "picture of modern philosophy as centered in epistemology and driven by the desire to ground our representations."[2] In place of this standard narrative of a philosophical quest for foundations on which to rest cognitive certainty, Neiman proposes that "the problem of evil is the guiding force of modern thought."[3] She argues that, "as an organizing principle for the history of philosophy, the problem of evil is better than alternatives. It is more inclusive, comprehending a greater number of texts; more faithful to their authors' stated intentions; and more interesting."[4]

This displacement of epistemology from center stage in the history of modern philosophy is complementary to a major thesis that Taylor advances in *Sources of the Self* with respect to the intellectual dynamics that surround the emergence of the buffered self of modernity. He argues that the engine that drives the disembedding of the self from the structured forms of social relationality characteristic of premodernity is principally a moral one, but that the moral locus of its origin has been significantly occluded by the dominance of interpretations that focus on the epistemic consequences of that disembedding rather than on the ethical motivations that have driven it. Taylor, moreover, enriches this

2 Susan Neiman, *Evil in Modern Thought: An Alternative History of Philosophy* (Princeton: Princeton University Press, 2002), 5.

3 Neiman, *Evil in Modern Thought*, 2–3.

4 See Neiman, *Evil in Modern Thought*, 7, where she further elucidates how it is "more interesting": "Here interest is not merely an aesthetic category, important as that is, but also an explanatory one, which answers Kant's question: What drives pure reason to efforts that seem to have neither ends nor results?"

thesis in an important way in *A Secular Age* in that his argument in the later work locates the dominance of such interpretations as itself part of the constellation of elements that have given rise to the immanent frame as social imaginary of secularity. Taylor and Neiman thus both see a moral drive as central to the forces that have given the human world its secular shape and its concomitant construal of human identity in terms of a buffered self. They also each note, though in different ways, how the secular shape it has taken has, ironically and all too often tragically, placed blinders upon our capacities to acknowledge the moral character of that drive. This obscuring of the moral dynamic at work in the shaping of the cultures of secularity has consequences that bear upon the project of articulating a theological anthropology for discerning the working of grace in those cultures. The most important of these consequences bear upon the scope of the self-understanding of our agency and the conditions of its exercise that we bring to efforts to comply appropriately to the exigencies of that moral drive. As will be discussed in more detail in chapter 5, we have often rendered ourselves insensitive and inattentive to the morally constitutive dimensions of the socially embedded finitude of our agency that constitute the locus of our receptivity to invitations to participate in the enactment of grace in and for the fractured world in which we dwell.

Whereas Neiman's first thesis offers a claim that is primarily historical, her second thesis then articulates what gives the problem of evil its conceptual and practical "traction"—that is, what makes grappling with evil the point at which "ethics and metaphysics, epistemology and aesthetics meet, collide and throw up their hands."[5] Neiman's thesis here—not a modest one—is that "at issue [in the problem of evil] are questions about what the world must be like for us to think and act within it."[6] She continues, "It is fundamentally a problem about the intelligibility

5 Neiman, *Evil in Modern Thought*, 5.
6 Neiman, *Evil in Modern Thought*, 5.

of the world as a whole."[7] Not only is she straightforward about affirming the ineluctably metaphysical character of the problem of evil—"when the world is not as it should be, we begin is ask why."[8] She goes so far as to describe metaphysics as fundamentally indexed to the problem of evil: It is "the drive to make very general sense of the world in the face of the fact that things go intolerably wrong."[9] In this she provides a crucially important gloss upon two of Kant's claims that play key roles in the account he gives of human agency and that will provide an important point of reference later for construing our human receptivity to grace; one is the ineluctability of the human "disposition" to metaphysics; the second is the primacy of the practical use of reason. Each of these functions as a marker of the finitude of our agency that is the locus of our receptivity to the invitation to participate in the enactment of grace.

Neiman builds her historical case for the first thesis on an astute remapping of texts from Leibniz to Rawls. In place of terrain traditionally apportioned among rationalists and empiricists on the farther side of the Kantian critical divide, with the major post-Kantian settlements in late modernity eventually deployed into foundationalist and anti-foundationalist camps, she offers a line of demarcation traced by reference to the problem of evil along which to place philosophers of the modern and nascent postmodern eras.[10] On one side are those for whom "morality demands that we make evil fully intelligible"; Leibniz, Pope, Rousseau, Kant, Hegel, and Marx stand here.[11] On the other are "those for whom morality demands that we don't"; here stand Bayle, Voltaire, Hume, Sade, and Schopenhauer.[12] She recognizes

7 Neiman, *Evil in Modern Thought*, 7–8.

8 Neiman, *Evil in Modern Thought*, 322.

9 Neiman, *Evil in Modern Thought*, 322.

10 Her chronological starting point is 1697, the publication date of Bayle's *Dictionary*, which she takes to mark the beginning of the Enlightenment.

11 Neiman, *Evil in Modern Thought*, 8.

12 Neiman, *Evil in Modern Thought*, 8.

that there are important figures—notably Nietzsche and Freud—who don't neatly fall in place on either side of this line. Nietzsche, on his part, shows a stubborn allegiance to both camps,[13] while Freud denies the distinction between natural and moral evil, which took firm hold on the intellectual terrain in the aftermath of the Enlightenment's paradigm marker of evil, the Lisbon earthquake of 1755.[14] Neiman argues that our own contemporary paradigm marker of evil, Auschwitz, has fully shattered not only the distinction between natural and moral evil—which provided much of the energy for modern religious and secular theodicies—but all other conceptual resources deployed for dealing with evil since the Enlightenment.[15] Following Levinas, she argues that "Auschwitz destroyed two central responses to evil that can be viewed as secular theodicies."[16] The first response (Hegel's) "sought to redeem particular evils by placing them in history"; the second (Nietzsche's) "argued that the problem of evil is our own creation."[17]

Yet overturning Hegel and Nietzsche, she then argues, provides little comfort for those who may have thought that

13 Neiman, *Evil in Modern Thought*, 204: "Nobody was more vehement in denying the existence of an order behind appearances, or in denouncing the attempt to find one as a denial of life. Yet nobody struggled harder against passively accepting appearances, nor warned more actively against nihilism."

14 Neiman, *Evil in Modern Thought*, 237: "The older Freud was at once the most articulate proposer of naturalism and the author of one of the darker views of human nature. It is thus little surprise that principled distinctions between different kinds of evil melt away in his work. They are all merely instances of countless ways in which life is too hard for us: the whole world presents obstacles to thwart our desires."

15 Neiman's use of Auschwitz as an exemplary marker of the exhaustion of modern conceptual resources for rendering evil intelligible does not rest upon claims about its *uniqueness* in the annals of mass murder, be it in terms of the number of its victims, or the cruelty with which those murders were done. See Neiman, *Evil in Modern Thought*, 256: "If whatever is new about contemporary evil cannot be simply a matter of relative quantity, neither is it a matter of relative cruelty."

16 Neiman, *Evil in Modern Thought*, 240.

17 Neiman, *Evil in Modern Thought*, 257.

placing the full responsibility for evil on human intent had decisively banished theodicy: "Auschwitz [also] undermined the modern rejection of theodicy that locates evil in intention."[18] In short, even as "Auschwitz threatens to undermine the modern determination to live without theodicy ... it devastated modern attempts to replace it."[19] Neiman's account of philosophy undertaken in the shadow of Auschwitz is thus cast in terms of a reflection on the claim made by Levinas that "perhaps the most revolutionary fact of the twentieth century consciousness ... is the destruction of all balance between explicit and implicit theodicy of Western thought."[20] She seeks to construe this claim in light of the fact that "elements of traditional discussion of the problem of evil have reemerged in response to Auschwitz."[21] She thus offers a sketch of the efforts of thinkers she considers representative of post–World War II philosophy—Camus, Arendt, Adorno and Horkheiemer, and Rawls—to grapple with questions of evil, even though they do so "in painful awareness that even the attempt to voice them may be problematic."[22]

While Neiman's reading of modern philosophy is impressive enough as a tour de force upon the terrain of the intellectual history of modern culture, its more fundamental import lies in reorienting our conceptual focus upon the dynamics of modernity in order to see the full scope of the challenge contained in her second thesis. In articulating her case for this second thesis— that the problem of evil "is fundamentally a problem about the

18 Neiman, *Evil in Modern Thought*, 240. Neiman notes the general silence of much twentieth-century philosophy on the problem of evil: "If any one feature distinguishes twentieth-century philosophy from its predecessors, it is the absence of explicit discussion of the problem of evil" (*Evil in Modern Thought*, 288).

19 Neiman, *Evil in Modern Thought*, 258.

20 Emmanuel Levinas, "Useless Suffering," in *The Provocation of Levinas: Rethinking the Other*, ed. Robert Bernasconi and David Wood (London: Routledge, 1988), 161. Quoted in Neiman, *Evil in Modern Thought*, 238.

21 Neiman, *Evil in Modern Thought*, 291

22 Neiman, *Evil in Modern Thought*, 291.

intelligibility of the world as a whole"[23]—she lays out the contours of the intellectual and moral dynamics that place the question of evil not merely at the center of modern philosophical inquiry but as implicated in each of our efforts to make sense of our humanity and the place of our humanity in the world. According to this thesis, evil brings into fundamental question what Neiman sees as the unbreakable connection that our human efforts to make sense of the world seek to forge with our hope of being at home in a world that has been, in modernity and its aftermath, disenchanted of any expectation that it is there to welcome us. As she puts this point in more abstract terms, "Ethics and metaphysics are not *accidentally* connected. Whatever attempts we make to live rightly are attempts to live in the world."[24] Since, moreover, she takes our "attempts to live in the world" as thoroughly historical, the connection between metaphysics and ethics also encompasses history: There also is no such thing as metaphysically innocent history, and to the extent that humanity has responsibility in the shaping of history, humanity plays a crucial role in giving history its metaphysical stamp.

Neiman's rereading of the history of modern philosophy thus makes the case that evil poses questions about the intelligibility of the world even more basic than those that have been engaged under the heading of "the problem of evil" by the varied religious and secular forms of modern theodicy. Evil presents a problem so fundamental to the efforts of human reason to render the world intelligible—be they efforts of a reason disciplined to function within the self-imposed limits of a Kantian critique, or the all-encompassing reason of Hegelian dialectic, or the efforts of instrumental reason to trim the world down to serve whatever seems to be the most immediately pressing human purpose—that it makes the standard modern distinctions among the genres of philosophical inquiry break down. Neiman explains, "Every time we make the judgment *this ought not to have happened*, we are

23   Neiman, *Evil in Modern Thought*, 7–8.

24   Neiman, *Evil in Modern Thought*, 327.

stepping onto a path that leads straight to the problem of evil. Note that it is as little a moral problem as it is a theological one. One can call it the point at which ethics and metaphysics, epistemology and aesthetics meet, collide and throw up their hands. At issue are questions about what the structure of the world must be like for us to think and act within it."[25] Neiman thus sees the disenchantment of the world of nature, which functions as central to any construal of our human circumstances that we are able to make from within the immanent frame, as providing us with a deeply ruptured conceptual terrain from which we now must continue efforts to make sense of evil. The account that she gives of the attempts of philosophers from Bayle to Rawls and from Kant to Arendt to make sense of evil on that terrain does not accord the triumph of a definitive resolution to any of them. In fact, the attempts she thinks have made some contribution to comprehending evil are ones, such as those offered by Kant, Nietzsche, and Levinas, that show in starkest terms the intractability of the problem. The legacy they bequeath is not a resolution; it is, at its most urgent and incisive, the staking out of a number of important markers for orienting the efforts at *resistance to evil and repairing its effects*, efforts that have now become the common responsibility of a humanity made aware, in a time of secularity, of being as deeply fractured as the terrain on which it dwells.

25 Neiman, *Evil in Modern Thought*, 5, emphasis in original. Cf. KprV AA 5:146–48/Cam 257–58 ("On the Wise Adaptation of the Human Being's Cognitive Faculties to his Practical Vocation") for one text in which Kant engages the issue of "what the structure of the world must be like for us to think and act in it" in a way that suggests the aptness of Neiman's characterization of the problem of evil as "the point at which ethics and metaphysics, epistemology and aesthetics meet, collide and throw up their hands." Kant argues here that if the moral structure of the world were transparent to the theoretical use of human reason, it would become impossible for us to lead morally worthy lives; we would do what is right in view of the reward we know accrues to it, rather than in view of recognizing that its rightness makes it fit for us to do. This is part of what Neiman calls "one of his greater arguments: if we knew that God existed, freedom and virtue would disappear" (Neiman, *Evil in Modern Thought*, 327). Cf. CPR, A 818–19/B 846–47.

Neiman offers two tropes to orient us, first, to what the fractured world in which humanity is situated in the aftermath of modernity "is like" and, second, to the manner in which we must "think and act within" that world. The first trope—which stands for what the world "is like"—is "homeless." She offers this to frame our human circumstances of a "conceptual helplessness" in the face of evil that seems to have taken intellectual hold in the aftermath of the massive horrors that humans have inflicted on each other since at least the start of the twentieth century—and continue to do so in the twenty-first. As the next section will elucidate, this trope provides a striking characterization of an important inflection that the self-understanding of human-buffered identity takes under the circumstances in which the contingency of uncertain outcome presents itself within the naturalistic constraints of the immanent frame. It also bears directly upon how we construe the socially situated consti-tution of our agency and the fundamental form of the human relationality in which we are called upon to be enactors of grace. This latter dimension of Neiman's trope will be treated in more detail in the next two chapters, in concert with George Steiner's complementary trope of being "guests to one another."[26] Each of these figures draws attention to the importance of the welcoming of others and otherness, of an inclusive human hospitality, as prime locus for enacting "grace"—a hospitality that, by its expansive, all-encompassing embrace, addresses and begins to heal the fractured circumstances of a fractured humanity in the immanent frame.

Neiman's second trope—which stands for how we must "think and act" in the world—is the insistent "Why?" of a child's questioning. She offers this as a model for the hope in which we are called to persist as we seek our human way through the inhos-pitable terrain of a disenchanted world that unstintingly presses us with the challenge: Why, in the face of the intractable resistance

26 Theo Hobson, "On Being a Perfect Guest: The Tablet Interview: George Steiner," *The Tablet* 259 (August 13, 2005): 15.

evil presents to human efforts to render it intelligible is it all the more important—indeed, even necessary—for the integrity of our humanity to persist in those efforts?[27] The reason that Neiman proposes to justify such persistence—"To abandon the attempt to comprehend evil is to abandon every basis for confronting it, in thought as in practice"[28]—is more than an expression of a moral concern that, if we cease to engage in intellectual efforts to make sense of evil, we eventually will falter and ultimately fail in our moral efforts to resist, repair, and overcome it. At stake in the question of evil are all our efforts to render intelligible the world that we engage both in thought and in action. We need to identify what stands as our most fundamental human recourse against the power that evil has—as unintelligible surd, adamantly resistant to efforts to exact sense from it—to shatter our efforts to make sense of the world and to fracture into disarray whatever hope we may have to give meaning to our human lives.

These two tropes thus function in her account of evil as coordinates for locating, first, the source of the fault line that evil exposes as running through human experience and, second, the dynamics that shape the contours of that line as it confronts the exercise of finite, embodied human freedom within the contingency of the spatio-temporal world. The fault line demarcates the fracturing of human intents, purposes, and meanings as they move athwart the radical contingency that, as Neiman notes, the workings of nature present to us as the context in which we strive to make sense of the world and to satisfy our aims within it: "Our power over the consequences of our actions is really very small."[29] She continues, "The gap between our purposes and a nature that is indifferent to them leaves the world with an almost

---

27 See R AA 6:47–51/Cam 91–95; KU AA 5:450–53/Cam 316–18 for two important texts in which Kant underscores how the sustaining of moral effort is a function of a hope originating in the recognition of the "moral vocation" we have in virtue of our freedom.

28 Neiman, *Evil in Modern Thought*, 325.

29 Neiman, *Evil in Modern Thought*, 74.

unacceptable structure."[30] Neiman's second trope will also have an important role to play in the later articulation I will be providing, in chapters 5 and 6, of the "transformative seeing" by which we are empowered in grace to enact, for and with one another in our fractured world, the shared hope envisioned in such transformative seeing. Before my argument can move on to this discussion, there remains a need to provide further coordinates upon the workings of the contingency in which our human efforts to make sense of the world and of ourselves, as well as to live and act within that world, are situated.

THINGS GONE WRONG: CONTINGENCY IN CREATION

"The problems of our relative helplessness in the face of contingency arise whether we are thinking of moral evils or natural ones. For the former are an instance of the latter: we are one of the things that go wrong with the world."[31]

My discussion has previously noted that a distinction between two "inflections" of contingency will be of major consequence for constructing this anthropology of situated human freedom. A

30 Neiman, *Evil in Modern Thought*, 75. In the *Critique of the Power of Judgment*, Kant articulates this gap in terms of a "righteous" unbeliever (explicitly mentioning Spinoza) who experiences the indifference of nature even to persistent human moral efforts (KU AA 5:452/Cam 317–18): "But his effort is limited; and from nature he can, to be sure, expect some contingent assistance here and there, but never a law-like agreement in accordance with constant rules (like his internal maxims are and must be) with the ends to act in behalf of which he still feels himself bound and impelled. Deceit, violence and envy will always surround him, even though he is himself honest, peaceable and benevolent; and the righteous ones besides himself that he will encounter will, in spite of all their worthiness to be happy, nevertheless be subject by nature, which pays no attention to all that, to all the evils of poverty, illness and untimely death, just like all the other animals on earth and will always remain thus until one wide grave engulfs them all together (whether honest or dishonest, it makes no difference here) and flings them, who were capable of having believed themselves to be the final end of creation, back into the abyss of the purposeless chaos of matter from which they were drawn."

31 Neiman, *Evil in Modern Thought*, 91.

more extensive account of that distinction is now in order for the purpose of spelling out its bearing upon the tension that arises within the construal that the immanent frame is constrained to offer, on the basis of its naturalistic presuppositions, both of what it is to be human and of circumstances in which the human is situated. After offering an overview of this key distinction, the rest of this chapter will then focus on a more detailed exposition of the second inflection—the contingency of uncertain outcome—in view of its importance for identifying the deep instabilities within the construal that the immanent frame leads us to make of our humanity and of our human circumstances. The next chapter then will focus on the first inflection—the contingency of creation— and elucidate the bearing that the interplay of both inflections has for construing our human circumstances and the makeup of our humanity in ways that are more adequate than what is provided by the immanent frame. Within the interplay of both inflections, our embodied human vulnerability will emerge, first, as a locus within which the tensions within the immanent frame become particularly manifest and, second, as a vantage point from which we are invited to discern grace working in the fractured circumstances of our human condition.

The first inflection of contingency is the one that articulates the contingency *of* creation—that is, the original gratuity of God's bringing to be the entire creation of which the human is part. The second inflection articulates the contingency operating *in* creation—that is, the dynamics of the created order that mark out the finitude of the scope and efficacy of the human agency exercised in that order. This first inflection renders the contingency of creation theologically as the sustained primal enactment of grace—good freely bestowed from and enacted by God's abundant inner goodness.[32] As David Burrell has argued, a mature theological articulation of the contingency of creation

32 See David Burrell, "Creation as Original Grace," in *God, Grace and Creation*, ed. Philip J. Rossi (Maryknoll, NY: Orbis, 2010), 99: "Avowing that the origin of the universe is free means, of course, that it is an utterly gratuitous act of God, a grace."

emerged from a long process of reflection within the traditions of Abrahamic monotheism.[33] Central to this way of understanding the originating of the cosmos—in contrast to Hellenic speculative accounts of necessary emanation from an eternal principle—is its characterization of the Creator's freedom in bringing creation to be: "Creating fills no need in God and so is an utterly spontaneous and gracious act."[34] This theological account of the contingency of creation thus marks not only the radical dependence within which the cosmos stands—that is, it is not self-originating—but also the gracious free abundance out of which it is brought to be, sustained, and brought to completion.

The contingency functioning *within* the primal enactment of grace that is creation, however, is one that, in contrast, is inflected—particularly with respect to human agency—as a "contingency of uncertain outcome." This is the contingency of what might have been different, a contingency often manifest as a contingency of fracture, of events and outcomes that could—and should—have been otherwise but were not, of "things gone wrong," in consequence of dynamics of nature as well as the enmeshment of human agency in the webs of multiple contingencies in the workings of a created world standing totally in radical dependence.[35] As a result, an adequate philosophical or theological parsing of the differences between these two "inflections" of contingency must keep their uses in proper relation to one other. It requires that its account of (the grammars of) divine and human freedom serve a dual function that enables us, first, to recognize— with respect to each inflection—the radical difference between divine and human agency and, second, to articulate appropriate ways, notwithstanding that difference, for characterizing their

33 David Burrell, *Freedom and Creation in Three Traditions* (Notre Dame, IN: Notre Dame University Press, 1993).

34 Burrell, *Freedom and Creation in Three Traditions*, 8.

35 Following the trajectory of Neiman's account, this should *not* be taken as aligned with the way modernity has inflected a distinction between "natural evil" and "moral evil; see Neiman, *Evil in Modern Thought*, 267–88.

relationship to each other. It is this difference and this relationship that provides the locus for elucidating a syntax for speaking intelligibly of grace and of the human receptivity in which it is enacted; this difference and relationship will be of particular importance for understanding how human vulnerability constitutes a fitting locus from which and in which grace is enacted.

The contingency *of* the world's creation—that in its entirety and that in each and all of its parts it is *at all* (for, inasmuch as "creating fills no need in God," creation simply might never have been)—may evoke wonder and praise and provide occasions for awe, reverence, and delight, but matters seem to stand quite differently with contingency encountered *within* creation. Contingency encountered *in* creation—that events and things go amiss and, far too often, go dreadfully wrong—is occasion for bewilderment, fear, sadness, despair, and rage. Contingency in creation is unsettling not simply by seeming random or capricious in how it befalls us; it is unsettling all the more by the fact that, when things go amiss, we can envision how they "might have been otherwise"—particularly when the "otherwise" seems to be what had been, but no longer is, within the scope of human action and control ("If only I had done this rather than that"). Unlike the contingency of creation, for which the counter-possibility of utterly nothing at all strains the limits of imagination, thought, and language, we *can* readily imagine, think, and speak of many possibilities of how it might have been otherwise when things go wrong in the workings of contingency in creation— and perhaps no more so than when we are enmeshed in contingency in ways that make us participants in its agency.[36]

The heightened awareness of the contingency of uncertain outcome in the world that is disenchanted brings in its wake a varied set of human responses. One response of particular import

36 Neiman's striking interpretation of Kant's oft criticized essay, "On a Supposed Right to Lie from Altruistic Motives," usually read as a not very convincing defense of exceptionless moral principles, takes it instead to make a point about our relation to the deep contingency of our actions, a point that "we have no wish to hear: our power over the consequences of our actions is really very small." Neiman, *Evil in Modern Thought*, 73–74.

with respect to our own self-understanding in such a world is a corresponding awareness of the depth and extent of our human *vulnerability* in the face of the workings of that contingency. In the context of the central role that instrumental reason has been accorded by the immanent frame for shaping our response to the workings of the world, it is not surprising that *gaining control of the workings of the world* emerges as a core strategy for protecting our vulnerabilities against the ravages of things gone wrong. Yet, as both Taylor and Neiman point out, much of the testimony of the human history that has unfolded in the wake of increasing human instrumental capacity to direct and alter the workings of the world to human purposes seems to belie the promise of overcoming the contingencies that heedlessly impinge upon our vulnerabilities. Our efforts to ward off such impingement all too often bring in their wake further impingements—and those latter may be of at least as much consequence as the ones we originally hoped to ward off.

Neiman offers an astute gloss on the human ambition in a disenchanted world to have the kind of control over the forces affecting our lives that once could only be imagined as a divine prerogative. On her account, such a wish to play God does not, in the first instance, stem from a will to exercise omnipotent power on one's own behalf. It arises instead from an experiential apprehension of the depth to which contingency, as it escapes both our capacity for understanding and the control of our finite agency, shapes the trajectory of our lives. Neiman writes, "Yet the wish to determine the world can't be coherently limited, for you cannot know which event will turn out to be not just another event, but the one that will change your life."[37] She continues, "The wish to be God isn't simply pathological; its alternative is blind trust in the world to work as it should."[38]

Neiman's trope of "homeless" is especially telling for capturing how the confidence modernity once had in our human

37 Neiman, *Evil in Modern Thought*, 74.
38 Neiman, *Evil in Modern Thought*, 75.

powers to render the world more fit for our human dwelling has been so thoroughly shattered. The powers of instrumental reason were envisioned, in the name and guise of "progress," as the almost ineluctable and even the well-deserved consequence of successfully explaining, in increasingly greater extent and detail, both the workings of nature and our human place in those workings. She argues that, despite the heroic efforts of so many modern thinkers, from Leibniz to Rawls and from Bayle to Camus, to wrest sense from the world—and, most importantly, to make sense of our human place in the workings of that world—the outcome has fallen tragically short of expectations. The disenchantment of the world has become all the more plainly seen in its full consequences: Since purpose is not part of the world's working, the world most assuredly is not made for our welcome—and all too often, *we* then add our human patterns of unwelcome to nature's indifference. Humanity, in consequence of the thoughtlessness of the evil it has all too often wrought upon itself and upon the surrounding world, has rendered itself more and more "homeless" in the world.[39] Betterment in some circumstances of human living has come at high, even exorbitant, cost that is all too often paid by further degradation of the circumstances of human living of those who have shared little in its betterment. Those who are most vulnerable all too often are the ones on whom even heavier burdens are placed. Having first disenchanted the workings of the world of nature into indifference to human purposes—often in the hope that those purposes might then have more full play— we have proved ourselves no better than an indifferent nature at clearing space upon which to welcome one another's flourishing.

In consequence, the conditions of human life two decades into the twenty-first century provide us little from which we may find firm assurance that we have yet learned how to make the space on which we dwell a fitting "home" for one another as

39 The thoughtlessness with which we humans do evil is pointedly expressed in the cover illustration of Neiman's *Evil in Modern Thought*: Francisco Goya's 1797 etching, *El sueño de la razon produce monstruos* (The sleep of reason produces monsters).

fellow humans, let alone for other living beings with whom we share the earth. The workings of the world of nature provide little guarantee—and we seem to provide even less to one another in the social worlds we construct to affirm "our" identity over against "their" identity—that we have mastered the skills to share, in a modicum of peace, even some little space side by side with those fellow human beings whom we perceive as not "us." It has also started to become more apparent that even modest expectations we may have about our own security and the well-being of the generations to succeed us may fail to be satisfied on a planet on which the effects of our resource-depleting human modes of living increasingly crowd out and even render uninhabitable the life space of many fellow creatures. The rendering uninhabitable of our own life space has already started to loom, not only as ominously close, but also in forms likely to lie beyond the capacities of human instrumental control.

ABANDONED SELVES
IN THE SPACES OF CONTINGENCY

The picture I have so far sketched on the basis of the accounts that Neiman and Taylor provide of the fractured landscape within which humanity finds itself dwelling in the aftermath of modernity has been in most respects a bleak one. The bleakness in these accounts stems from the tension they identify in the interplay between the unrelieved naturalist inflection in which contingency is articulated and the drive within our human self-understanding to make sense of where and how we stand within the workings of contingency. When the workings of contingency upon humanity and its circumstances are articulated in the naturalist register, the various forms of human vulnerability upon which contingency impinges stand as just one general fact among the set of elements constituting our human situatedness and upon which instrumental reason may be employed for direction and control. At the same time, that register offers no basis for construing the fact of our vulnerability—or, for that matter, any other fact of our circumstances—as bearing particular significance for understanding what it is to be human in a world of contingency, inasmuch as the drive to make sense must be construed as itself one more "fact."

So from the naturalist perspective of the immanent frame, Neiman's trope of "homeless" may put the fact of our vulnerability into an affective register, but neither that register, nor this specific trope, offers a basis from which to give an orientation to the work of instrumental reason in efforts to direct or control the impingement of contingency upon our vulnerabilities. The trope may provide a negative inflection upon the way we might see the indifference that the workings of the world have toward our human purposes and aspirations, but, in the end, its affective tenor offers nothing normative for guiding any effort we might then undertake for dealing with what we take to be the effects of that indifference. Indeed, with respect to this naturalist construal of the workings of contingency, the drive to make moral sense of a world rife with the indifferent play of contingency that gives bite to the trope of "homeless" may itself be otherwise understood as hopelessly ineffectual as reason itself. It is just one more instantiation of a vulnerability peculiar to the ambitions of human reason that can best be diagnosed in accord with the Humean dictum that reason is slave to the passions.

On that diagnosis, one might be well advised to distance oneself from futile efforts to render the play of contingency upon human vulnerability morally intelligible by taking on a neo-Lucretian sensibility of the kind given elegant expression in the work of Hume. That sensibility is succinctly captured in a remark of Neiman's: "Where it's only a matter of knowledge, the fact that what affects us is not created by us causes little problem."[40] In a world of contingency in which the only intelligibility consists in "one damn thing after another" over which our control can be, at

---

40 Neiman, *Evil in Modern Thought*, 80.

best, intermittent and local, prudent self-interest and measured moral sympathy both suggest that a quest for moral intelligibility that extends beyond the scope of human customs that serve to bring about external social harmony is, at best, idle.

Taking the indifference of the workings of the world to our human purposes as simply a basic fact about the world thus provides a basis for a "realism" about our human circumstances and moral capacities. This "realism" is one for which Thrasymachus in Plato's *Republic*, Machiavelli, Hobbes, and Hume have provided expression of some of its more recurrent variants, but it hardly provides a stable coordinate from which to orient the workings of our instrumental reason for anything more than an occasional and equally contingent amelioration of some particular vulnerabilities.[41] Knowing that the workings of an indifferent contingency can impinge on any and all of our vulnerabilities does not give instrumental reason a point from which to determine *which* of these vulnerabilities, if any, should be the focus for efforts to devise ways to ward off or to minimize the effects of the impingements of contingency. Even more profoundly unsettling is that the acknowledgment of this fact about the indifferent workings of contingency provides even less guidance with respect to *whose* vulnerabilities should be given priority in the protective endeavors of instrumental reason.

The "realism" that the immanent frame suggests is the best that we can settle for in negotiating our human way through contingency is thus a moral posture that both Neiman and Taylor find to be considerably less than adequate to measure up to what they take to be an adequate understanding of what it means to be human. For Taylor, such realism advises the "prudent strategy" of managing the tension between awareness of standing deeply vulnerable to the vicissitudes of the world's indifferent contingency and the drive to make sense of that vulnerability "by stifling the

41 See Neiman, *Moral Clarity: A Guide for Grown-Up Idealists* (Orlando: Harcourt, 2008), 124–45, for a provocative discussion of the moral limits of "realism."

response in us to some of the deeper and most powerful spiritual aspirations that human beings have conceived."[42] It entails what he calls "spiritual lobotomy": a strategy of self-induced amnesia of the spiritual in the name of getting on with life.[43] For Neiman, it is the "realism" that is "a form of sloth. If you tell yourself that a world without injustice is a childish wish fantasy, you have no obligation to work toward it."[44] Such realism entails abandoning the hope that she sees as a central part of the moral heritage of the Enlightenment, one for which Kant provided a particularly powerful expression in his articulation of the regulative function of reason that demands the persistent exercise of our agency to *make* an otherwise indifferent and even resistant world into a morally intelligible world. As she reads Kant's account, whatever *moral* purposes we may think are necessary for our making sense of the world are not features *of* the world but rather a *demand* that our reason *brings to* the world. Neiman writes, "Belief that the world should be rational is the basis of every attempt to make it so . . . the demand that reason and reality come to meet is the source of whatever progress occurs in actually bringing them together. Without such a demand, we would never feel outrage— nor assume the responsibility for change to which outrage sometimes leads."[45] So contrary to a realism that would contract the human moral horizon, neither Taylor nor Neiman consider the fractured circumstances in which we dwell in the aftermath of modernity to constitute a condition that requires humanity to scale back significantly or even to abandon a robust hope for living rightly in the world, a hope they each see emerging from the deepest resources within what constitutes us as human.

In Taylor's case, this hope takes its form in aspirations that he denominates as spiritual; these aspirations are indicative of a fundamental human dynamism in the interpretation we make of

42 Taylor, *Sources of the Self*, 519.

43 Taylor, *Sources of the Self*, 520.

44 Neiman, *Moral Clarity*, 145.

45 Neiman, *Evil in Modern Thought*, 325–26.

ourselves as situated in the space of moral meaning. In the context of the social imaginary provided by the immanent frame, he attaches particular import to what he calls "languages of personal resonance" as loci for a "seeing good" that empowers a moral hope that extends beyond the reductive naturalistic parameters set by the immanent frame.[46] As we shall see in the next chapter, the very origin of these languages of personal resonance as part of the emergence of the immanent frame makes them all the more potent as an element in the tension placing pressure upon the immanent frame's account of the human.

In Neiman's case, this hope also emerges from a fundamental human dynamism that seeks to render the world intelligible in all its dimensions, but a dynamism that faces a seemingly insuperable challenge from the contingency of evil that presses upon moral space in which we dwell and interact with one another. In professed alliance with Kant, she locates this moral demand for making evil intelligible as a function of our rationality. Making sense of the world—even when it resists our efforts—is fundamental for our human dealings with the world. "We are so structured as to expect a world that comes to meet us halfway, for we cannot make meaning alone.... Belief that there may be reason in the world is a condition of possibility of our being able to go on in it."[47]

Taylor and Neiman thus stand in agreement that any adequate account of what it is to be human requires affirming hope as the central mode of empowerment for thoughtful human moral engagement with the world. Such hope bears upon both how we think and how we act in the multiple dimensions in which we engage the world and engage one another in that world. They further agree that, when read solely from an optic that construes humanity's enmeshment in the workings of the world to be fully

---

46 Taylor, *Sources of the Self*, 502–21; see Philip Rossi, "Divine Transcendence and the 'Languages of Personal Resonance,'" in *Theology and Conversation*, ed. J. Haers and P. DeMey (Leuven: Peeters, 2004), 783–94.

47 Neiman, *Evil in Modern Thought*, 233–34.

explicable in the naturalistic terms set by the immanent frame, the physical, moral, and social circumstances in which humanity dwells in the early twenty-first century seem to offer slender ground for hope. It is not simply that the explanatory principles of the immanent frame provide little basis for now hoping that a hitherto indifferent nature has been rendered more amenable through the efforts of instrumental reason to bend it to human purposes. It is also that whatever slender grounds for hope offered by the immanent frame need to confront this deeply ironic fact: The circumstances in which human life is now situated, particularly many of those with potential to wreak widespread social, economic, environmental, and physical dislocation affecting larger populations, are themselves the outcome of the uses to which humanity has put instrumental reason. This suggests that humanity has little reason for taking itself to be a vessel sturdy enough to bear the hopes of its own, often only intermittent, best aspirations, let alone to be an agent of such hopes.

Yet, in spite of the seemingly unrelieved bleakness in which they describe the landscape of fracture that constitutes the human condition in the aftermath of modernity, Neiman and Taylor both affirm hope as central to humanity's efforts to live with integrity and respect for one another on such a landscape. They both also understand such hope to be efficacious—it is neither wishful thinking nor unreflective optimism, but a hope that, as it looks unblinkingly upon the landscape of human fracture, is able, in Neiman's phrase, to give "attention to the pieces"[48] in ways that enable us to clear space to dwell with one another even upon the fractured landscape that had hitherto rendered us "homeless." They also both locate hope as a constitutive dynamic of what it is to be human; it is of no little significance for the articulation of a situated anthropology of grace that their accounts of this dynamic present it, though in different ways, as inscribed in human vulnerability.

For Neiman, the vulnerability out of which hope arises is marked out by the persistent "Why?" with which a child seeks to

48 Neiman, *Evil in Modern Thought*, 326.

understand the workings of the world and that stands as a trope for the "principle of sufficient reason" inscribed in the human quest to make sense of the world. She points out that for Kant, unlike Leibniz, the principle of sufficient reason "cannot be a fact about the world but a demand on it."[49] Behind the persistent "Why?" lies the demand that for "*everything that happens, find the reason why it happened this way rather than that.*"[50] Kant's understanding of the moral import of this demand upon the practical agency of human reason provides key conceptual coordinates for Neiman's account of both the sturdiness and the fragility of this quest and the hope that arises from it. As she succinctly puts it: "*What we are* is beside the point here, for nothing we do will reveal our real essence. What most matters is *what we should be*. Hence we ought to hold whatever view of nature, and progress, best supports that. What's the minimum we need to believe about the goodness of the world in order to contribute to making it better?"[51]

For Taylor, it is a hope he finds manifest in the paradoxically decentering expressivism of late nineteenth- and early twentieth-century art and literature, which he characterizes as "immanent revolt" against the naturalistic strictures that the immanent frame places upon "depth" of meaning.[52] The expressivism found in the work of authors such Rilke, Proust, and Pound, or in artists such as Cezanne, counters in a distinctively modern way the flattening that ensues from reductive naturalism. Their work manifests a sensibility attentive to an "epiphanic" dimension in which the world discloses itself in the space of humanity's inward engagement with the world. The epiphanic provides a space in which "both decentering and inwardness are fully recognized."[53] The genealogy that Taylor provides of this expressivism and its coordination in modernity to the epiphanic

49 Neiman, *Moral Clarity*, 201.

50 Neiman, *Moral Clarity*, 190, emphasis in original.

51 Neiman, *Moral Clarity*, 276.

52 Taylor, *Sources of the Self*, 456–93.

53 Taylor, *Sources of the Self*, 482.

helps to uncover its theological lineage, which as the next chapter will explore is embedded in an expressive understanding of the utterance of the words that in Hebrew scripture are the very manner of God's creating.

The link that Taylor provides between the expressivism that has emerged within the immanent frame and a theological construal of creation that long antedates it will thus provide an initial step for setting forth the role that hope, as constitutive of the makeup and the understanding of the human, plays in a theological anthropology of situated freedom. To do this, my discussion can now turn to an account of what was noted earlier as the "second" inflection of contingency. This is the contingency *of* creation, the contingency that marks the radical dependence of creation upon the original gratuity of God's bringing to be and sustaining the entire creation of which the human is part. Placing the contingency that is operative in creation—that is, the contingency of uncertain outcome—within the contingency of creation as a whole—that is, the contingency of radical dependence—will thus be the first of the reorientations that I will be proposing in the course of the next three chapters for enlarging the horizon of the immanent frame so that space may be opened for discerning the workings of grace in the fractured spaces of contingency.

Chapter 4

Creation:
Enacted Space of Divine Hospitality

THE IMMANENT FRAME AS THE SPACE
OF CONTESTED FREEDOM

AS THE SOCIAL IMAGINARY OF secularity, the immanent frame would have us envision our "social existence, how [we] fit together with others, how things go on between us and [our] fellows, the expectations which are normally met, and the deeper normative notions and images that underlie these expectations"[1] as taking place in a world that has been "disenchanted." Such a world goes its way devoid of the operation of any inner purposes and lacks, as well, any direction from powers or forces whose workings cannot be rendered explicable from the constructive activities of human intelligence functioning within the confines of what is empirically accessible and measurable. The previous chapters have argued that an important consequence that follows from such disenchantment is the concomitant priority that the immanent frame gives to instrumental reason in the construal it offers of what it is to be human and the circumstances in which humanity finds itself. Whatever "direction" that may come from the workings of the world—for example, its physical or biochemical processes from the smallest scale to the complexities of evolution—is "blind"; that

1 Charles Taylor, *A Secular Age* (Cambridge, MA: Belknap Press of Harvard University Press, 2007), 171.

is, it is devoid of any reflective intent or purposive direction from the world and its elements. In consequence, any purpose that gives order or direction to our human engagement with the world can arise only in virtue of the control we humans can wrest from the world by the devising of our instrumental reason.

The blank face that a world without its own purposes presents to us is fundamental to Neiman's perception that a disenchanted world renders us "homeless": we are left to our own devices—which, in the end, themselves are part of a disenchanted nature—to figure out how to dwell with one another in a world that runs its course in utter indifference to individual or common weal or woe. A disenchanted world provides no assurance that the dominance, let alone the survival, of our species will persist beyond a few more seconds, let alone minutes, on the cosmic and geological time scales that measure out the life and the death of planet earth. Nonetheless, in accord with what Taylor has termed "subtraction narratives" in which the emergence of secularity is a function of scientific knowledge replacing religion as the regnant explanatory paradigm, the disenchantment that has rendered nature void of inner purpose is taken to be a straightforwardly positive outcome of the increasing scope of scientific knowledge of the workings of nature and the correlative capacities for human technological control that such knowledge empowers. Modernity's discovery of nature's lack of purpose thus makes it a ripe field for the play—and for the conflict—of human purposes. At least one variant of such subtraction narratives, espoused particularly by those whom Taylor has named the "boosters" of modernity, takes the increase of human instrumental control over the full range of human life circumstances to befit our human makeup: a world not made "for us" in *its* intent (for the world can have none) is one that now provides us with the opportunity for shaping it in accord with intents and efforts of *our* human agency.

Dissent from such a positive picture for the prospects and eventual outcome of greater human control over the workings of the world is not a recent development in modernity nor one that has simply been occasioned by more recent attention to the large- and small-scale harmful consequences that have ensued for the environment from the often heedless and sometimes deliberate misuses of the human capacities to control the workings of the world. There are deeper conceptual roots to such dissent, the most powerful of which are founded upon careful attention to the limits that experience and reflection manifest as constitutive elements in the structure and functioning of human agency operating within a world of natural contingency and in interaction with the agency of other humans. So even as some major currents of the intellectual and cultural movement that saw itself as the harbinger of increasing enlightenment proposed that humanity was capable of charting and enacting an ever upward trajectory for itself, there were voices both within and outside that movement that urged caution; such optimism was unrealistically and even dangerously uncritical about what could and what would result from the exercise of an expanding human control over nature, including over humanity as itself ingredient in, and an outcome of, the workings of nature.

This dissent has often been sharp and trenchant, notably so when articulating the recurrent form of imaginative depictions of dystopian cultures that might arise in consequence from the overreach of human ambitions or uses of instrumental reason to reshape society that is heedless of unintended or unforeseen consequences. The power of such depictions often issues from the attention they give to the ways in which the disenchantment of the natural world repositions humanity not only in relation to the workings of nature but also in relation to the structures and dynamics of human society. This dissent suggests a further vector along which the contingency of uncertain outcome creates tension within an all-too-rosy construal that the immanent frame might encourage us to make of our humanity and of its power to alter our human circumstances. Along this vector lie important questions about the bearing of human freedom upon the relationality embedded in the structure of our humanity and how human freedom and human relationality together then stand in relation to the instrumental use of reason that, from the perspective of the immanent frame, is the single resource humanity has available for dealing with "things gone wrong" in a world of disenchanted contingency.

Kant is one of the "dissenters" from a view that has unconditioned confidence that the increased capacity of human instrumental reason to bend nature to human purposes will be sufficient to bring about the conditions that make it possible for humanity to attain the definitive state of human well-being that he terms "the highest good." Kant's cautions about confusing rationally founded hope with uncritical optimism in our human engagement with the world have already been noted. His caution on this matter provides useful pointers for delimiting the manner in which humanity's engagement with a disenchanted world needs to be shaped from a self-understanding that appropriately recognizes and enacts the good that is appropriate to the finite, fragile, and fractured place in which humanity is situated in the cosmos.

It is thus of no little importance for the task of articulating an adequate account of the human that his caution about the confidence we may justifiably place in our human capacity to shape the world to our purposes arises from his acute perception of a moral self-opaqueness deeply rooted in human agency. He calls this moral opaqueness "radical evil," and he finds it all the more intractable inasmuch as it functions in a world that is disenchanted. This is so because the disenchantment of the world, on Kant's account, is not simply a fact about the world devoid of moral import. It is rather an aspect of our human relation to the world fraught with moral import inasmuch as it requires us to articulate our human place in the cosmos precisely in terms of the moral purpose our finite situatedness serves in that disenchanted world. In terms of Neiman's striking claim, grasping the human import of the disenchantment of the world not only makes it manifest that "ethics and metaphysics are not accidentally connected"—but also that it is in and upon our humanity itself that such a connection has its deepest import.[2]

So even as Kant views our human attribution of purpose to the workings of the world as necessary to structure our scientific investigation of the world, he also clearly affirms that a world so investigated is disenchanted: It is a world for which the necessity of such an attribution of purpose is "subjective." By this he means that its origin is not drawn from the world but is structured into the finite mode of cognition with which we engage the world. Though purpose is necessarily a part of *how* we make judgments about the working of the world, we cannot thereby claim that purpose is, in fact, *a feature of* the inner workings of the world—in Kant's terminology, we cannot claim that it is the way the world works "in-itself." So even as Kant labors in texts such as the *Critique of the Power of Judgment*, as well as his occasional essays on history, politics and culture, to legitimate the application of categories of purpose to the workings of nature, that legitimation is not put forth as the basis for a claim about how the world "is": Whatever purposes, if any, the world of nature may have as it "is"—"in-itself"—remain opaque in principle to the theoretical use of finite human reason.[3] In consequence, whatever purposes may be operative in the workings of nature remain equally opaque to the instrumental use of reason, inasmuch as its orientation—at least as this is construed from within the immanent frame—comes from coordinates provided by the theoretical use of reason.

2 Susan Neiman, *Evil in Modern Thought: An Alternative History of Philosophy* (Princeton: Princeton University Press, 2002), 327.

3 Cf. "First Introduction to the Critique of Judgment" (EE) AA 5:181–86/ Cam 68–73, especially 186–87/Cam 72: "The power of judgment thus also has itself an *a priori* principle for the possibility of nature, though only in a subjective respect by means of which it prescribes a law, not to nature (as autonomy), but to itself (as heautonomy) for reflection on nature, which one could call the *law of the specification of nature* with regard to its empirical laws, which it does not cognize in nature *a priori* but rather assumes in behalf of an order of nature cognizable for our understanding in the division that it makes of its universal laws when it would subordinate a manifold of particular laws to these" (emphasis in original).

Kant's account of the attribution of purposes in the working of the world, however, is not confined to its role in the theoretical knowledge that provides a basis for human instrumental intervention upon the operations of nature. Understanding the function of moral purposes in the structure of human agency is of far greater weight in his account of what it is to be human in a disenchanted world: Such purposes are fundamental for making moral sense of the world and of our human place within it. Since a disenchanted world is devoid of its own purposes, human moral purposes have a crucial role to play in giving the world a moral trajectory. These purposes are thus ordered to the formation and direction of human action in and upon the world, but the human action so formed is not shaped and governed in the mode of instrumental reason shaping the world to serve contingent human purposes. Such action is shaped and governed instead in the mode he calls reason's "practical"—that is, moral—use of reason. It is thus the practical use of reason that enables us to shape the human world so that it provides the conditions requisite for the mutual exercise of human freedom—or, in Kant's own terminology, the conditions requisite to establish a "kingdom of ends" or an "ethical commonwealth."[4]

In Kant's account of radical evil and the human finite freedom that forms its context, the world thus presents itself as *both* morally and theoretically disenchanted: Whatever purposes we may think are necessary for our making moral sense of the world are not features *of* the world but rather a demand our reason *brings to* the world. Bringing to the world as it "is"—devoid of purpose—the demand of practical reason to fashion the world as it "ought to be"—as locus for the mutual exercise of moral freedom—is central to what Kant affirms as the primacy of the practical use of reason.[5]

4 See Philip J. Rossi, *The Ethical Commonwealth in History: Peace-Making as the Moral Vocation of Humanity* (Cambridge: Cambridge University Press, 2019), 14–20.

5 Important affirmations of the primacy of practical reason can be found in both CPR, "The Canon of Pure Reason," Second Section, A804–19/B832–47, and CprR, AA 5:119–21/Cam 236–38.

Reason brings those purposes to the world not in the mode of theoretical knowledge and instrumental reason but in the mode of a practical (moral) hope that, by heeding the dictate of practical reason to do as we ought, makes it possible for us to envision and enact a moral order for human interaction in a world that would otherwise be devoid of such an order.

This moral order envisioned by practical hope is thus one in which we enact for one another the space and conditions for the mutual exercise of our human freedom. Yet such enactment takes place in the context of a disenchanted world in which the contingency of uncertain outcome, of things that "go wrong," provides the only available field for human mutual engagement. On such a field, if we take seriously the blank indifference that its disenchantment presents to us, we will find that it offers a place for human interaction most aptly characterized as an arena of contention, competition, and conflict, a locus in which the contestations of a Hobbesian state of nature get repeatedly played out. It is thus not accidental that, within the disenchanted world envisioned in the social imaginary of the immanent frame, forms of "social contract" have played a major role in efforts to account for the formation, functioning, and authority of institutions governing human social relations.

A disenchanted world thus provides no level playing field for the engagement of human freedom with human mutuality. Within the workings of the contingency of uncertain outcome the contestations of divergent human purposes and the clash of human freedoms play themselves out in the form of zero-sum games, in which losers frequently far outnumber winners, and even seemingly consistent winners have little assurance about the next outcome. The contingency of uncertain outcome in the disenchanted world of a culture of secularity thus functions in a way that is ironically similar to what the enchanted world of ancient Greeks saw as the interplay among the iron hand of necessity, the capriciousness of the gods, and the human overreaching they termed "hubris": Despite all our human hopes, purposes, and intentions, these forces are the ultimate determinants of the trajectory and outcome of our human lives. We may have greater confidence than the Greeks did in the power and the worth of human autonomy in a world that goes its own way and may take some comfort from seeing the impingement of its forces upon us as coming from its blind indifference rather than the capricious or malicious intent of the gods, but the outcome is the same: Of all the indifferent, capricious, blind, willful, malicious impingements of the world, death provides the definitive marker that, for all our posturing and protest, the world has its relentless and iron way with us.

Among the tensions and ironies in the account that the immanent frame constrains us to give of our humanity and our human condition, this may be the one that puts the greatest pressure upon its conceptual and imaginative coherence. On the one hand, the immanent frame—particularly as it has most recently been inflected in terms of the interlocking idioms of democratically governed polities and of market-driven postindustrial global capitalism—places human freedom, exercised as individual choice in the social, cultural, political, and economic spheres into which modernity has differentiated human activity, at the center of human self-understanding. An ever-widening array of objects that one may choose—from gadgets to lifestyles—is taken as the mark of an expanding horizon for the exercise of human freedom, even as this exponential proliferation of such objects also ironically underlines growing disparities in the wealth requisite for the very possibility of exercising such choices.

On the other hand, the world of nature from which human beings emerged and within whose workings their lives are enmeshed has been further "disenchanted" by human depredations that have unthinkingly taken nature as merely instrumental to human purposes. It is becoming increasingly clear that such destructive consequences of this instrumentalization of nature threaten to render ultimately pointless the exercise of human choice or of any other feature of human life and activity that has been claimed to make humans distinctive, if not unique, among the living species that have emerged from the workings of nature on our planet. In such a doubly disenchanted world, the human place in nature—despite the narratives about the self-importance of our species that we have been wont to give of ourselves in many variants in the course of human history—becomes very small indeed. Despite all our posturing about the power that instrumental reason provides to shape the world to our purposes, we have, in the end, little control over the contingencies at work in the world. In these circumstances Neiman's remark has a particularly ironic bite: "Our power over the consequences of our actions is really very small.... The gap between our purposes and a nature that is indifferent to them leaves the world with an almost unacceptable structure."[6]

This tension that the disenchantment of the world creates for the understanding that the immanent frame constrains us to give of the place and the function of human freedom—that it is at once the core of what it is to be human even as it stands as ultimately ineffective in the face of an indifferent cosmos in which our common fate is death—provides the background for the discussion offered in the next section. This discussion will propose a way for understanding and engaging the contingency of uncertain outcome, of things going wrong, that recognizes the world as a disenchanted world but also reimagines the significance of that world and its workings with reference to a more fundamental inflection of contingency. This other inflection is the contingency of the free origination of all that is from the divine gratuity that is marked out by what the three Abrahamic traditions of monotheism have articulated as the doctrine of creation. Even though the naturalist veto of the immanent frame mutes this inflection of contingency almost to a point of inaudibility, I will be proposing that its resonances may not be fully stilled even in a disenchanted world. The locus in which their sounding may yet be discerned arises from the pressure that our fractured world

6 Neiman, *Evil in Modern Thought*, 74–75.

places upon the severely truncated account of human freedom that the immanent frame constrains us to give. What that account cannot encompass is the horizon for moral intelligibility that *the ordering of human freedom demands of us—namely, an ordering to the enactment of the human mutuality that is appropriate to finite, self-reflective rational agents in a fractured world.*

Neiman's trope of "homeless" is particularly apt for locating human mutuality as enacted in freedom as the point at which this pressure is most intense. Construing our humanity in this way from the vantage of the immanent frame gives no basis for thinking that our recognition that a disenchanted world does not welcome us thereby empowers—or, more radically, even enjoins—us to welcome one another. Such empowerment has no stable basis within the immanent frame inasmuch as the mutuality from which it arises can be only be construed instrumentally in terms of an order of mutual benefit. Such a world offers welcome to none of us, but I may be willing to welcome you, provided doing so will make me welcomed in turn. Yet even this shared recognition that a disenchanted world provides a common estate that offers welcome to none of us is insufficient to overturn the zero-sum contention that fuels the Hobbesian dynamic of social relationality embedded in the immanent frame.

From this pressure point, it would seem that only dissonant resonances registering the bleakness of disenchantment are likely to be heard. I will suggest, however, that even within such discord there are possibilities for discerning elements that hint at tones from a profoundly different register. I will be arguing that these possibilities rest upon a parsing of the discourse of creation in ways that manifest, as a fundamental structure of its syntax, that *the enactment and empowerment of mutuality is a fundamental form of the gracing that God's creating brings about in and for the world.* Such "gracing," so this claim runs, inscribes a dynamic of mutuality as an orienting principle into and for the exercise of our human agency. To the extent that this dynamic of mutuality is inscribed in human agency, the discord discernable from the pressure that the realization of our "homeless" human condition places upon the immanent frame's construal of what it is to be human may be heard not merely in plaintive registers of despair and fury; it may also be heard as echoing the invitation of the dynamic of a graced creating inviting us into the enactment of mutuality. Listening for and recognizing that echo, however, requires first attending to those elements of the theological discourse about "creation" that voice, in the idiom of radical contingency, the abundant, unconstrained graciousness of God with which and from which the otherness that is creation has its origin, is sustained, and is inscribed in mutuality.

THE GRATUITY OF CREATION AND THE CONTINGENCY OF RADICAL DEPENDENCE

"All religion, all theology could be defined as an endeavor to grasp, to offer thanks for, the gratuitous miracle of creation," writes George Steiner.[7]

In their efforts to understand the cosmos in relation to the divine mystery that the Abrahamic traditions confessed as its ground and origin, Jewish, Christian, and Muslim thinkers engaged one another as well as the variegated inheritance of other cosmological speculation—principally, but not exclusively, Hellenic.[8] As David Burrell recounts that process, finding an appropriate way to conceptualize the manner of God's *acting freely* in creating was crucial for forging an understanding of the relation that creation bears to its Creator in a way that properly respects

7 George Steiner, *Grammars of Creation* (New Haven, CT: Yale University Press, 2001), 128.

8 See David Burrell, *Freedom and Creation in Three Traditions* (Notre Dame, IN: Notre Dame University Press, 1993), and *Knowing the Unknowable God: Ibn-Sina, Maimonides, Aquinas* (Notre Dame, IN: University of Notre Dame Press, 1986). Burrell recognizes that efforts to understand this relation long antedated the medieval interchange among the three traditions that Maimonides, Ibn-Sina, and Aquinas represent. He focuses on that interchange because he takes it to have forged a grammar for that relationship both more appropriate than any preceding it and still useful in contemporary contexts.

the radical difference between them.[9] The affirmation of creation *ex nihilo* provides one important marker of that difference: It notes that "the most radical sort of beginning" constituted in and by God's creating is "one that is utterly free on the part of the originator, and so cannot even be said to be received so originating is it."[10] Further, the *manner* in which creation is freely enacted marks the unique character of this acting as *divine* acting: It is radically different from any form of acting *in* that world to which the divine creating gives origin. The fundamental activity of divine creating is not an acting done upon what is preexistent to the acting. It is not a *poesis* of "production" bringing forth from what already is, but rather a radical originating that brings forth "the to-be of each existing thing," a phrase with which Burrell explicates *esse*, the term Aquinas uses to "express the effect proper to the first and most universal cause which is God."[11] Burrell provides a concise articulation of these points as follows:

> *Creation* means the free origination of all from the one God, who gains nothing thereby. Moreover, what the notion of *free* primarily concerns is the lack of any constraint, even a *natural* constraint; so it need not involve *choice*, as it spontaneously does for us, except quite secondarily. That creating fills no need in God and so is an utterly spontaneous and gracious act: that is the cumulative message of the scriptures appropriated by Maimonides and Aquinas. Everything else, including the apparent description in Genesis of an initial moment for the created universe, is secondary to that assertion.[12]

9 Following Robert Sokolowski in *The God of Faith and Reason* (Washington, DC: The Catholic University of America Press, 1995), 31–40, Burrell can call this radical difference between God and the world a "Christian distinction." See also Burrell, *Knowing the Unknowable God*, 75–78, 88–89.

10 Burrell, *Freedom and Creation*, 26.

11 See Burrell, *Knowing the Unknowable God*, 94.

12 Burrell, *Freedom and Creation*, 8, emphases in original.

Burrell takes Aquinas's articulation of the affirmation of God's acting freely in creation in terms of *esse* to be a major accomplishment that issues from an extended argument that thinkers in the traditions of Abrahamic monotheism had with "the necessary emanation scheme of neoplatonism."[13] Aquinas's achievement is significant, on Burrell's account, in view of the fact that, in the intellectual cultures that were the matrices for the formative conceptual articulations of the Abrahamic tradition's affirmation of God's free creation, emanation stood as "the principal contender to a revealed world view."[14] That view took it to be the case that creation issued of necessity from God. When such claims about the necessary emanation of the world from the divine are placed over against the account of its origination from the abundant gratuity of God that was formed in the matrix of the three Abrahamic traditions, important issues arise about the distinctions that may be appropriately drawn between the created world and its divine originator. Neoplatonic emanationist accounts may no longer be highly visible contenders against the revealed worldview that Burrell sees articulated in Aquinas's treatment of the doctrine of creation. It is, however, at least arguable that claims and criticisms about the extent to which "onto-theology" has been a constitutive feature of modern theism can be also rendered as claims that key elements of such emanationist accounts have remain deeply inscribed in Christian theological traditions.[15] The larger point

---

13 Burrell, *Freedom and Creation*, 8.

14 Burrell, *Freedom and Creation*, 8.

15 To the extent that Aquinas is claimed to have played a prominent role in setting the trajectory of onto-theology, a criticism made by (among others) Paul Tillich, there has been a serious misconstrual of his thinking. See Michael Buckley, *Denying and Disclosing God: The Ambiguous Progress of Modern Atheism* (New Haven, CT: Yale University Press, 2004), 48–69. While Buckley's discussion focuses on ways in which this claim misconstrues Aquinas's account of how humans come to know God, it can be further argued that embedded in this epistemic misunderstanding is a metaphysical one that does not grasp the manner in which Aquinas's notion of *esse* functions in his articulation of the difference between the Creator and creation.

about the bearing that different accounts of "the origination of all" and the manner of its originating have upon the distinction between the world and its Creator, however, remains all the more valid in reference to accounts of "the origination of all" that are taken to be counter to the doctrine of creation. These have most often transposed the Neoplatonic necessary emanation of the world into an adventitious factuality amenable to explication solely within the naturalistic parameters of the immanent frame.

Burrell's recounting of the articulation of the doctrine of creation as it culminates in the syntax of *esse* that Aquinas fashions is formally about the metaphysical contours of that doctrine. What I will be exploring in the remainder of this section will be in keeping with Neiman's dictum that "ethics and metaphysics are not accidentally connected"[16] and my gloss upon her dictum that it is in and upon our humanity that a connection between ethics and metaphysics has its deepest import. In this instance, I will be considering the bearing that taking creation in the way that Burrell characterizes it—that is, as the "most radical sort of beginning" from out of the abundant gratuity of God—has for understanding our humanity and the circumstances in which we are situated, and for then understanding what is then required of us as moral agents. This discussion will propose that the idiom of the radical contingency of creation—when parsed as the abundant, unconstrained graciousness of God with which and from which the abundant otherness that is creation has its origin and is sustained—bears in a fundamental way upon our human self-understanding. Under this parsing, the radical contingency of creation stands as an invitation to exercise our freedom in the abundant mutuality of welcoming one another and all creation in all of its and all of our otherness. I will then further argue in chapters 5 and 6 that, in the cultures of secularity, the transparency and completeness of our human response to that invitation to mutual hospitality provides a primary locus for discerning the enactment of the empowering and transformative activity of grace.

16 Neiman, *Evil in Modern Thought*, 27.

Creation, apprehended as gifted in its entirety, unique and singular, and understood as Steiner's "gratuitous miracle," displays the enacted graciousness of God to which fitting responses are wonder, thanks, and praise. The contingency of creation presents a face that allows us to recognize how all that is and the abundant otherness of all that is—including ourselves—radically stands within a frame of an unasked-for dependence.[17] Apprehending that this contingency of creation in its character as radically originated dependence pertains to all that is as a whole, as well as to every space of its particularity and otherness, manifests the thoroughness with which our own human finitude is deeply embedded in that contingency. As thus doubly part of the contingency of creation, our finitude may itself be approached as an object of reverence, a reverence evoked by attention to the radical possibility that we simply might not have been—*that we are at all* is unasked for, and it is so in multiple ways. It is not just that creation need not have been at all; it is also that neither humanity as species, nor any of us as instances of our species, need have emerged as elements in that creation.

Viewed from the perspective of the immanent frame, however, what I have termed the unasked-for character of creation is most likely to be construed as sheer adventitious factuality that, of itself, ultimately has no point save whatever we make of it. Whatever significance the world may have as the sheer fact of "being there" in virtue of whatever complex interplay of intra-worldly causality has brought about its present state is not given with it. In this, the "break of the covenant [of meaning] between word and world" that in Steiner's judgment "defines modernity itself" is writ in largest terms.[18] Not only are things in and of the world devoid of any significance that issues from their inner constitution, but the world as a whole is itself similarly void.

17 In the context in which I am using it, "dependence" is to be understood in terms of a judgment about the entirety of all that is, not simply about one's own status.

18 George Steiner, *Real Presences* (Chicago: University of Chicago Press, 1989), 93.

If it is to have significance at all, that will arise as a function of whatever we may be able to make of it through the use of instrumental reason. Even as the world goes its "own way"—a way that we have become adept at charting, but a way which the naturalist veto forbids us to ascribe any recognizable intent or purpose— it provides material (quite often recalcitrant material) for us to inscribe our own human purposes on it.

Consigning the unasked-for character of the world in which we are situated to the status of sheer facticity, however, has not been the only response possible from within the immanent frame. Another mode of response has been shaped by the varied forms of what Taylor calls "the immanent revolt" against a naturalistic flattening of the world and its import into whatever instrumental reason can press into service for human purposes. This revolt took one form in the Romanticism of the nineteenth century that was an effort to read back into the inner workings of nature some elements of intrinsic significance that had been driven out by the disenchantment effected through the demise of the teleology of final causes and the dominance of instrumental reason. It is, however, the later emergence within this immanent revolt of what Taylor terms "expressivism" that particularly manifests how the immanent frame's construal of agency itself begins to press against the consignment of the world as a whole and all of its workings of the world to mere facticity.

What makes expressivism significant is that, on Taylor's account, as it takes form in the literary and artistic works that bring forth "the epiphanies of modernism," it places double pressure on the naturalistic parameters of the immanent frame. The pressure comes from both the subjective and the objective sides of human self-understanding engaging the world. One side of this pressure issues from expressivism's understanding of the receptivity to meaning at the core of human subjectivity. The other side of this pressure arises from expressivism's presentation of the profoundly decentering character of encountering the world in ways that allow things in and of the world to manifest themselves in full otherness. There is an ironic character to these pressures inasmuch as expressivism itself has a fully modern lineage: both the subjective and the objective sides of expressivism arise from forces that are constitutive of the immanent frame. Expressivism renders the dynamic of their interaction in human self-understanding in ways that Taylor takes to indicate the persistence of a spiritual thrust within human agency that the immanent frame has otherwise made mostly invisible.[19] Beyond these pressures, moreover, the immanent revolt has further significance for the central role I have already indicated for human vulnerability in discerning the workings of grace in the cultures of secularity: Whether or not one is willing to speak of it as "spiritual," there is a dynamic of discernment of what it is to be human at work in both the artistic and the conceptual modes of the immanent revolt. Through its dynamic of discernment, expressivism has thus played a role in drawing attention to human vulnerability and fragility as key sites of "fissure" in and for the immanent frame. In marking vulnerability as crucial to the discernment of what constitutes us as human, these rebellious offspring of the immanent frame help to identify and stake out a vantage point from which possibilities for grace may at least be glimpsed.

Taylor's account of the dynamics of the immanent revolt against the naturalistic strictures of the immanent frame and the emergence of expressivism provides one indication that forms of reverence, awe, and even praise before the unasked-for character of creation continue to function, albeit in transformed ways, in the cultures of secularity. Neiman's trope of the child's persistent posing of the question "Why?" in almost every circumstance as well as the link she sees between the relentless quest for intelligibility and our capacity for moral outrage is another. "Belief that the world should be rational is the basis of every attempt to make is so. . . . Without such a demand, we would never feel outrage—nor

19 See Charles Taylor, *Sources of the Self: The Making of the Modern Identity* (Cambridge, MA: Harvard University Press, 1989), 419–93; *Secular Age*, 594–617.

assume the responsibility for change to which outrage sometimes leads."[20] Her remark about the evocation of moral outrage from things gone wrong in the world is particularly helpful in that it helps us take note that, in a culture of secularity, the modes into which reverence and awe in the face of the unasked-for character of creation are often transformed, make it challenging to discern them clearly at work in our engagement with the world.

Such transformation, as well as the difficulties it presents for seeing the awe and reverence that nonetheless still shape it, may itself be an outcome of a profoundly disorienting element that, not surprisingly, is inscribed in the recognition of the contingency of radically originated dependence. This contingency is marked by a unique relation in which all that is and whatever is stand in radical dependence with respect to the originative priority of that which is their source.[21] What is disorienting about this relation is that it both manifests the radical nonreciprocity of otherness in which creation stands to its Creator and is informed by an equally radical mutuality of presence, the radical mutuality captured in Augustine's expression, *Deus intimior intimo meo.*[22] Articulating this relation poses a complex imaginative, conceptual, and linguistic challenge. Burrell observes that "the relation between

---

20 Neiman, *Evil in Modern Thought*, 326–27.

21 See David Burrell, "Creation as Original Grace," in *God, Grace and Creation*, ed. Philip J. Rossi (Maryknoll, NY: Orbis, 2010), 104: "If creator and creature were distinct from each other in an ordinary way, the relation—even one of dependence—could not be non-reciprocal; for ordinarily the fact that something depends from an originating agent, as a child from a parent, must mark a difference in that agent itself. Yet the fact that a cause of being, properly speaking, is not affected by causing all-that-is does not imply remoteness or uncaring; indeed, quite the opposite. For such a One must cause in such a way as to be present in each creature as that to which it is oriented in its very existing. In that sense, this One cannot be considered as *other* than what it creates, in an ordinary sense of that term; just as the creature's *esse-ad* assures that it cannot *be* separately from its source."

22 "[You] were more inward than the most inward place of my heart" (Augustine, *Confessions*, trans. F. J. Sheed [Indianapolis: Hackett, 2006], bk. 3, ch. 6).

this One and all that is created cannot be likened to a relation among created things, forcing us to search for a way of articulating its uniqueness, so leading us ineluctably to 'negative theology,' of which there are several varieties."[23] One way we might attend to the radicality of this dependence is the extent that we allow ourselves to enter the conceptually vertiginous metaphysical wonder of Leibniz's question, "Why is there something rather than nothing?" We further gesture at the uniqueness of this relation when we grapple with the difficulty of imagining there being "nothing at all," as well as when we ponder the *aporiai* that, since at least as far back as Parmenides, have constantly beset efforts to articulate a syntax for speaking of what, in contrast to all that is or might be, (absolutely) "is not."[24]

In consequence, to the extent that the unasked-for contingency of radically originated dependence can be, even fleetingly, recognized as presenting itself within the immanent frame as anything other than sheer facticity, it can have a doubly disorienting character for the social imaginary of the cultures of secularity. The first disorientation comes from the conceptual and imaginative challenge it presents as a relation that has no recognizable counterpart "in" or "of" the world. As Burrell's account indicates, forging a syntax to enunciate this relation in a way that appropriately marks its uniqueness without also being deeply misleading required centuries of reflective philosophical and theological labor. Even Aquinas's hard-won articulation of this unique relation into the language of the Creator's *esse* (and, as Burrell astutely points out, of creation's *esse-ad*) can (and has

---

23 David Burrell, "Creator/Creatures Relation: 'The Distinction' vs. 'Ontotheology,'" *Faith and Philosophy* 25, no. 2 (2008): 182.

24 The perplexities confronting both grammar and imagination in limning the contours of the "not" that delimits the radical contingency of creation have preoccupied some forms of philosophical and theological inquiry in late modernity. This presents opportunities for significant philosophical engagement with theological questions that, earlier in modernity, would be dismissed as, at best, the quaint residue of metaphysical perspectives of little credibility in an intellectual culture of empirical science and secularity.

been) all too readily be read as a key marker along the trajectory of drawing God into the ambit of the "ontotheological."[25] It is pressure from this first disorientation, arising at least as an implicit recognition of the contingency of radically originated dependence, that various forms of the immanent revolt make manifest as they push against the constrictive naturalism embedded in the immanent frame.

The pressure against restrictive naturalism that stems from the recognition of the contingency of radically originated dependence—a recognition embedded within the immanent revolt—can, however, be deflected by other important elements in the constellation of forces that have shaped the immanent frame and that stand in resistance to a recognition of radically originated dependence. These elements are, most notably, the social atomism that provides the grid for understanding human social relationality as primarily contractual and the instrumentalism that provides the paradigm for the form, functioning, and finality of the human inquiry that engages the world. It has already been suggested that each of these elements is invested in providing construals of the human within which the self is seen as disembedded from social relationality. In consequence, these elements, as discussion in the next chapter will indicate, carry within them an implicit denial that there can be a connection between ethics and metaphysics of a kind that, as Neiman claims, has significance for either our self-understanding or the exercise of the freedom that is constitutive of our rational moral agency.

This denial of the connection between ethics and metaphysics, implicit in the disembedding of the self from social relationality, stems from a construal of human relationality to otherness as one that is paradigmatically competitive and conflictual. Within this construal, the mutuality of recognition that gives structure to the moral world stands in tension

---

25 See Burrell, "Creator/Creatures Relation," 177–89, and "Creation as Original Grace," 104. Buckley's defense of Aquinas against the charge of being progenitor of the "ontotheological" is mentioned above, n. 15.

over against the (metaphysically) constitutive features of human agency as construed by social atomism. It is upon this tension that recognition of the contingency of radically originated dependence places a second disorienting pressure. This pressure arises inasmuch as *the otherness to which all relationality*—and especially the relationality of mutual recognition that is the orienting context for the exercise of human moral agency—*is ordered can be construed as itself a constitutive element of the radically originated dependence of creation.* This means that *to be a creature consists in being gifted into otherness*, an otherness that arises as the radical dependence of gratuitously offered origination. This mutual recognition of otherness, as it is both gratuitously offered and fully inscribed in creation, thus constitutes the moral world that provides the field for human interaction.

Taylor's affirmation of a "moral realism" provides one articulation of the way in which such otherness is inscribed in creation as marker for the moral orientation of human freedom. His moral realism disputes views claiming that the contingency of events in the world and self-determining human conduct are the only elements in the formative dynamics of human moral valuation and action. Against these views, he argues that structurally ingredient in the constitution of that moral field is also a set of constitutive goods, which he describes as "something the love of which empowers us to do good and be good."[26] These "strong moral sources" have a normative function that is both ethical and metaphysical.[27] This function arises from the "otherness" of the high demand they manifest, a demand that empowers the decentering of the self in its aspirations and that is fundamental to the dynamics of mutual recognition. These sources thus function as

26 Taylor, *Sources of the Self*, 93.

27 Although Taylor does not explicitly address the ways in which moral and metaphysical ordering intersect with one another, I believe that he would agree with Susan Neiman's dictum that "ethics and metaphysics are not *accidently* connected. Whatever attempts we make to live rightly are attempts to live in the world" (*Evil in Modern Thought*, 327).

normative by giving *a self-decentered direction to the self-determining activity of human freedom and agency.*

Taylor's moral realism is thus robustly teleological; its sources draw human conduct toward a "fullness" that, even as it encompasses human well-being in its totality, is not thereby determined exclusively or exhaustively by that well-being, nor brought about solely by self-determining human conduct. The normativity of these sources is also metaphysical. Taylor takes the fullness to which human activity is ordered to have its basis in that which can be appropriately affirmed not merely as an ideal moral horizon arising from the self-determining structure of human freedom. It is thus a genuinely transcendent reality, an empowering otherness that provides the exercise of freedom in human moral agency with a fundamental vector toward a fullness that is not merely of its own making.

These countervailing dynamics, empowered from nascent recognition of the contingency of radical dependence, place pressures upon the immanent frame from within. These pressures suggest that the awe, reverence, and wonder continue as powerfully appropriate forms of human response to this contingency, even as they are systemically provided little place within the social imaginary of the cultures of secularity. In a world within which social atomism and instrumental reason are regnant, such responses, which reflective traditions of religion and philosophy have long taken as expressive and formative for the core of our human self-understanding, have been neither displaced nor diminished, even as new forms of cultural distraction attempt to render them otiose. Yet, as Taylor's accounts of "immanent revolt," the "cross-pressures," and the "dilemmas" that persist across the landscape of the immanent frame make plain, there is even more import to these countervailing pressures than merely their continued persistence. They function, within the context of the challenges that the contingency of uncertain outcome presents to our human self-understanding and to our understanding of the disenchanted circumstances we inhabit, as markers of the hope that Taylor characterizes as the "central promise of a divine affirmation of the human, more total than humans can ever attain unaided."[28]

So, as discussion of the contingency of uncertain outcome, of things gone wrong, has already indicated, such responses of reverence, awe, and wonder also have to contend with the equally unbidden fact that our finitude means that, as the cosmos goes its course with us as part of it, the scope of our power and control is small indeed—and the powers we do have are ones we do not always use wisely or well. With this realization of the finitude of our human powers, moreover, each form of contingency presents another, more unsettling, face. We are now aware that "the starry skies above"—which Kant saw as one of the two referents worthy to evoke a response of awe from our finite human freedom—stretch billions of light-years beyond the horizon within which he and his age could place them.[29] We thus might be able to stand under those skies with awe possibly even greater than his before the fact that, as humans, we can claim no hand in the bringing forth and sustaining of the cosmos; such awe, in fact, might even provide a salutary humbling perspective upon what we take to be the accomplishments of our instrumental reason.

Yet learning more about the complexity of the cosmos from which our species has, on the scale of cosmic time, only recently emerged does not of itself make us more attentive of the extent to which far too much of what our species has wrought seems only to inflict scars upon our meager portion of that cosmos and upon the fellow beings with whom we share it as a common dwelling place. All too often where there has been much gain, there has been considerable loss; in fact, as we are now beginning to be increasingly aware, our use and consumption of the resources of our

28 Taylor, *Sources of the Self*, 521.

29 *Critique of Practical Reason* (CprR) in *Practical Philosophy: The Cambridge Edition of the Works of Immanuel Kant*, ed. Paul Guyer and Allen W. Wood (Cambridge: Cambridge University Press, 1996), 269–70. In the standard German edition (*Akademie Augabe*) of Kant's work, the passage is found at AA 5: 161–62.

planet is increasingly putting in peril processes that are essential to sustaining planetary life. In these circumstances, it seems legitimate to question the extent to which humanity remains justified in considering itself still capable of responding with equal awe before the other referent Kant places before our freedom: "the moral law within." Placed against the immensity of the cosmos in which our species has conducted itself more as intruder than welcomed guest, might we be well-advised, *contra* Kant, to be more modest than he in claiming awe as the proper measure of the worth of our human moral capacities and freedom?

CREATION AS KENOTIC HOSPITALITY

The next chapter will more directly engage the question just raised about the ways in which our human moral freedom can still remain a proper object of the awe in which Kant thinks we should hold it. This appears a particularly pressing question for an age of secularity that, as attentive as it may be to the pervasiveness of fracture in the human world, is regularly willing to settle for the kind of prudent moral "realism" that in the end will only tell us, in Neiman's trenchant phrase, that "a world without injustice is a childish wish fantasy."[30] As the discussion of the earlier parts of this chapter have indicated, the awe before the cosmos that Kant considers to be the coordinate marker of the unique human place in the cosmos remains possible. The significance of such a response, however, particularly with respect to its import for a structural (i.e., metaphysical) construal of what it is to be human and of our human condition, has become more problematic in view of key factors shaping the social imaginary of a secular culture—the naturalistic veto, the atomistic rendering of human sociality, and the hegemony of instrumental reason.

The concluding section of this chapter thus sets forth a perspective upon the contingency of radical dependence manifest

30 Susan Neiman, *Moral Clarity: A Guide for Grown-Up Idealists* (Orlando: Harcourt, 2008), 145.

in creation that, I will argue, provides an important repositioning of the contingency of uncertain outcome within the enactment of the contingency of radical dependence. Such repositioning, I will be arguing, helps to open possibilities for discerning the working of grace within the fractured human reality and the fractured circumstances of the disenchanted culture of secularity. My argument for this will be constructed on the basis of first bringing together two related strands in the work of Neiman and Steiner that help to chart a direction for dealing with the question of the human place—and the human task—in a cosmos that now bears, at least in the small part humanity inhabits, the scars of human fracture. To these two strands I will join a proposal for understanding creation as the contingency of radically originated dependence within a larger trajectory of Christian scripture that places humanity within a dynamic of the ongoing enactment of divine welcoming and hospitality that culminates with the kenotic entry of God into incarnate vulnerability in and to the world. This dynamic is one that unfolds from the gracious bringing of otherness to be that is creation, through the Incarnation of the Word into fully human vulnerability, to the Paschal transformation enacted in and by the Spirit that brings the good inscribed in all creation to its promised fullness. Creation may thus be construed as the space constituted by the originating hospitality of God in bringing it to be and sustaining it. Within this space of the radically originated dependence inscribed in creation, it is the recognition of our shared human vulnerability in the face of the contingency of uncertain outcome that stands open to receive a graced empowering of our human enactments of hospitality. These enactments thus become the kenotic form in which we participate with one another in the ongoing enactment of the creating, redeeming, and sanctifying hospitality of the God who entered fully into our human vulnerability.

The strands from Neiman and Steiner issue from the key tropes that they employ to convey the central moral demand placed upon our human relationality in the fractured condition humanity finds itself in the aftermath of modernity. Neiman's trope of "homeless" and Steiner's trope of learning to be guests to one another resonate contrapuntally with each other in depicting the dynamics of welcoming and rejection as a central modality for shaping humanity's response to the fractured circumstances in which it is placed and has placed itself in the aftermath of modernity. These tropes convey the central importance they each place upon the enactment of the mutual welcoming that makes space for us to be at home with one another in the world: Welcoming is fundamental to the very enactment of our humanity in that it creates the space for the mutuality that constitutes the moral world of our interaction with one another.

Reading these tropes as markers of the fundamental place that hospitality holds in the enactment of our humanity is particularly instructive when it is placed over against the scriptural trajectory of hospitality offered, rejected, but then more expansively reoffered. That hospitality is one that, even as it is rudely rebuffed, is not on that account then withdrawn but instead extraordinarily extended. That trajectory can be rendered in large theological brush strokes as one along which the divine-human relationship moves in the course of the drama of creation and salvation articulated in Christian scripture. A dynamic of hospitality offered and rejected is its very starting point. God's creation may itself be viewed as a divine "making room" into which to give welcome to the abundance of all that God creates. God, the most gracious host, invites the man and the woman, fashioned in God's very image, to make the garden, expressive of the abundance of God's whole creation, their dwelling place. Yet within that abundant hospitality, the man and the woman find a way to make themselves ungracious guests. Their expulsion from the garden brings in its wake all the forms of human inhospitality, starting with the brutal inversion in which fraternal invitation ("Let us go out to the field" [Genesis 4:8 RSV]) provides pretext for Cain to carry out his murderous design on the life of Abel, his brother. Large and small patterns of hospitality offered, often rejected, yet even when rejected offered again are deeply inscribed in the narratives of Hebrew scripture and the Christian New Testament.

This trajectory of hospitality offered, rejected, but then more expansively reoffered is displayed in the gospel narratives through the manner in which God, now come to dwell with us incarnate in Jesus, draws us beyond the threshold marked out by our human practices of inhospitality. From a birth for which there was no room in the inn, through a ministry in which many of his own, even of his family, received him not, to a death for which there was hasty burial in a borrowed tomb, the pattern of God's reversal of human inhospitality becomes more and more manifest. To each of these rejections, the ever-gracious God responds with a yet even more expansive and all-encompassing welcome: The Spirit that is poured out in and through the risen Christ now brings into being the Church as locus for ongoing enactment of the all-encompassing hospitality of God. In accord with the dynamics of the pattern displayed in the scriptural narratives, a key marker of such hospitality is its expansive renewal in response to rejection. In that expansive renewal, moreover, particular attention is paid to include within its scope those who otherwise have had no place of welcome. The Spirit of the incarnate and now risen God makes the new community a space of hospitality for those to whom the principalities and powers of the world have offered no welcome. The trajectory comes to its completion in the offering of yet one more dwelling place, "the holy city, the new Jerusalem, coming down out of heaven from God" (Revelation 21:2 RSV).

When it is placed in relation to the trajectory of hospitality traced in scripture, the hospitality that is affirmed by Neiman and Steiner as fundamental to the enactment of our humanity may even be seen, if not as itself an enactment of grace, as providing an opening toward the possibility of such enactment in a fractured and disenchanted world. While the conceptual and imaginative grammar they each provide for articulating the fractured terrain of modernity does not explicitly offer a syntax for a language of grace, it is of import that they each use the related language of "miracle" to underline the central role of what they each take to be central conceptual markers for our efforts to grapple with our human place in our fractured world. For Neiman, that marker is found in the relation between the real and the rational in which the contrast between the world as it is and the world as it ought to be is expressed: "If the events that determined the twentieth century left contemporary experience fractured, any conception of reason that can be salvaged must reflect fracture itself.... What binds the real and the rational together must be so fragile that it will seem miraculous—and on occasion the miracle occurs. As with any other miracle, it takes something like faith to perceive it."[31] Steiner characterizes the enactment of creation, which stands at the center of what he sees as the drama of modernity's struggle to wrest authority over meaning from God, as the "gratuitous miracle" that all religion and theology "endeavor to grasp, [and] to offer thanks for."[32] Their use of the language of miracle in their respective arguments may point to a theological subtext embedded in the important conceptual nexus they articulate; more important for my purposes, however, is that this conceptual nexus implicates a recognition that human freedom's capacity for the acknowledgment and enactment of mutuality provides a marker from which to discern the unasked-for, decentering invitation to and bestowal of the good of mutual recognition as a working of "grace."

For Neiman, the binding between the real and the rational that bridges the metaphysical rupture between the world as it is and the world as it ought to be is brought about in the exercise of human moral freedom. Following Kant, she sees such exercise as the practical use of reason, the use of human reason to which Kant gives priority in the functioning of a principle that lies at the heart of his critical project: the unity of the theoretical and the practical uses of our finite human reason that is necessary for our efforts to render intelligible the world that we engage both in

31 Neiman, *Evil and Modern Thought*, 327.

32 Steiner, *Grammars of Creation*, 128.

thought ("as it is") and in action ("as it ought to be").[33] The unity of reason provides our most fundamental human recourse against the power that evil has—as unintelligible surd, adamantly resistant to efforts to exact sense from it—to shatter our efforts to make sense of the world and to fracture into disarray whatever hope we may have to give meaning to our human lives.

For Steiner, the connection between creation as "gratuitous miracle" and human freedom is marked out in another trope that he uses to precipitate the multiple forms of gracious receptivity and welcome that he sees in play in the enactment of a work of art. This trope is *cortesia,* which he also renders as "tact of heart." He articulates the dimensions of *cortesia* primarily in reference to fashioning and encountering a work of art, human activities that, as proxies in modernity for the uniquely divine action of creation, have been a key locus of human efforts to wrest authority over meaning from God. His articulation frames this figure as rooted in a graciousness of bearing that should inform the freedom with which humans encounter not only a work of art but also one another: "Where two freedoms meet, where the integral liberty of donation or withholding of the work of art encounters our own liberty of reception or refusal, *cortesia*, what I have called tact of heart, is of the essence."[34] *Cortesia* thus stands for that human bearing in encounter with "the other" in which the "graced enactment" of a welcome empowers mutual reception.

Neiman and Steiner thus each make significant gestures that suggest that the mutual hospitality we offer one another in the disenchanted world that otherwise renders us "metaphysically

33 Cf. CPR, "The Canon of Pure Reason," esp. A795–819/B823–47, for Kant's articulation of the unity of reason at the outset of his critical project. As is the case for many of the keys aspects of that project, Kant revisits, refines, and reformulates his account at a number of later points. See Susan Neiman, *The Unity of Reason: Rereading Kant* (New York: Oxford University Press, 1994), for an account of the trajectory along which Kant's account moves.

34 Steiner, *Real Presences*, 155; he provides extensive treatment of this on 147–78.

homeless," the *cortesia* that should inform the mutual encounters of freedom, may be construed not simply as fundamental to the enactment of our humanity, but as an enactment that may even be construed as "graced." As graced, it is an enactment done from *the outpouring and reception of an inner abundance within the dynamics of human freedom.* When we then orient the construal that Neiman and Steiner provide of the significance of human hospitality for the very enactment of our humanity along the trajectory of hospitality found in scripture, it is my proposal that their construal of this inner abundance of hospitality offered and received may then be seen as even further, and even more fundamentally, graced. The scriptural trajectory is inscribed with the recognition and the affirmation that the most fundamental form of hospitality is in the divine enactment of creation as the original space of hospitality: Acknowledgment and acceptance of that radically originating offer of divine hospitality, creation itself, is condition for the very possibility of our human enactment of hospitality.

Another compelling set of observations from Neiman will provide the hinge upon which to turn from this discussion of creation as the enacted hospitality of God to the considerations offered in the next chapter about the central role that the recognition of human relationality as the matrix for the exercise of human freedom plays in the dynamics of enacted hospitality. These observations bear upon the depth of the fracture both within and without that marks human experience in a disenchanted world of secularity: "Where so many structures of modern thought have been shattered, whatever sense we find must be incomplete. Attention to the pieces is now all the more important."[35] She then adds, in view of the prospect that all our efforts to make sense of a fractured world are themselves so fragile that they will only come out as fragmented as we are: "Where experience was truly shattered, the pieces will never be neatly ordered again."[36] Neiman's remarks help to draw attention

35 Neiman, *Evil in Modern Thought*, 326.
36 Neiman, *Evil in Modern Thought*, 327.

to a central feature in the enactments of hospitality that most transparently manifest themselves as enactments of grace: They issue out of and in response to recognition of the shared human vulnerability upon which the workings of the contingency of uncertain outcome deeply impinge. My vulnerability encounters and engages your vulnerability, "our" vulnerability encounters and engages the vulnerability of "the other," in mutual enactments of welcome and reception.

Transposed into a theological idiom, Neiman's remarks bear directly upon the graced significance of the enacted hospitality that issues from the recognition of our shared human vulnerability in the face of contingency. In theological terms, "attention to the pieces," to the concrete vulnerabilities upon which contingency impinges, provides invitational space for participating in the enactment of grace that enables us to address our human vulnerability in concert with one another. Within such space, moreover, the invitation to participate in the enactment of grace draws attention to the deep commonality of our human vulnerability: Contingency is no respecter of persons. We all stand in need of being made welcome; we all have the capacity for offering welcome and receiving welcome from one another. In consequence, this space also invites recognition of the shared hope requisite for sustaining efforts to "gather the pieces" and to bring them together in due reverence for their fragility. In terms of Neiman's trope, we must have the kind of hope that makes it possible for us to "pick up the pieces" with and for one another. Hope thereby opens possibilities for enacting, in the first instance, that which reverences and treasures the remnants we are left with, as well as possibilities for envisioning ways to bring them to a renewed wholeness. Such hope enables us to envision and undertake these efforts as tasks we are called upon to share with one another in virtue of our common human vulnerability. As the next chapter will indicate, the hope that enables us to envision our human wholeness and to be participant in its attainment is founded on the recognition of mutuality that shapes the structure and the exercise of our human finite freedom.

Chapter 5

Autonomy, Vulnerability, and Otherness:
Locating Grace in the Worldly Spaces of Contingency

HORIZONS OF GRACE:
FREEDOM, MUTUALITY, AND VULNERABILITY

THIS CHAPTER WILL PROVIDE AN account of human freedom that focuses on its engagement with contingency in each of its inflections—the contingency of uncertain outcome and the contingency of radical dependence—that in concert give shape to our human condition and provide coordinates for our self-understanding of what it is to be human. Within the larger project of articulating an anthropology of situated human freedom to render the workings of grace intelligible in a culture of secularity, this account will function to establish that the recognition of human relationality serves as the fundamental matrix for the moral intelligibility and exercise of human freedom: *Human freedom is structurally situated within the relationality that constitutes us as moral agents with respect to one another.*

This relationality, I will then propose, situates freedom for then empowering enactments of hospitality fully open to the welcoming of otherness that respond appropriately to the disruptive and damaging impingements upon our human condition of shared vulnerability arising from the workings of the contingency of uncertain outcome. Such enactments of hospitality exhibit how the freedom of our human moral agency, when construed and exercised as structurally embedded in human mutuality, is empowered to engage the dynamics of human fracture and vulnerability. Such engagement marks out the interplay of fracture and vulnerability within the dynamics of worldly contingency that provides a space of openness to the workings of grace. This interplay between human vulnerability, human freedom, and human mutuality thus provides an important set of coordinates within the fractured circumstances of the culture of secularity from which it becomes possible to discern grace at work in the spaces of worldly contingency. Within these spaces of worldly contingency, as I will set forth in the final chapter, the contingency of radical dependence becomes manifest as the fundamental horizon of divine hospitality and accompaniment toward which the enactment of grace is oriented and from which it receives its intelligibility.

Within the history of Christian theological efforts to articulate the dimensions of grace, placing human freedom, human vulnerability, and human mutuality in relation to important aspects of the enactment of grace is by no means remarkable. In terms of an idiom (*gratia naturam perfecit*)[1] that has had long standing in that history, these designate aspects of the (human) nature that grace brings to completion. In the context of the cultures of secularity, however, the immanent frame has inflected freedom, vulnerability, and mutuality in ways that render them

---

1 Cf. Thomas Aquinas, *Summa Theologiae* I, q.1, 8 ad 2: "*gratia non tollat naturam, sed perficiat*"; I, q.62, a.5: "*gratia perficit naturam secundum modum naturae.*" For a provocative examination of this idiom, see Robert W. Jenson, "Gratia non tollit naturam sed perficit," *Pro Ecclesia* 25, no. 1 (2016): 44–52. The (expansive) translation he proposes in response to the question "How does God as grace perfect us?" is "He *envelopes* [sic] us with his perfect life" (52).

problematic with respect to the enactments of grace.[2] They are each circumscribed by the naturalist veto in ways that obscure the capacities they have, particularly in their relation to one another, that render them receptive to the empowerments of grace. As a result, one element in my argument, both in this and the next chapter, will be to take note of ways in which attention to the loci in which human freedom, vulnerability, and mutuality intersect often offers a more appropriate vantage point from which to discern their receptivity for workings of grace than do the ways that can be found by considering each one in abstraction from the others.

In this chapter, attention to their interaction will focus on the hope that arises in and for one another in the recognition of mutuality that shapes the structure and the exercise of our human finite freedom. Such recognition of the mutuality in which our freedom is embedded then enables us to envision, from out of our shared vulnerability and the fragments we are left with by the impingements of contingency, a human wholeness for which we are called to be participant with and for one another in its attainment. In the next chapter, attention to their interaction will then focus on the transformative, self-involving "seeing good" that empowers us to enactments of hospitality to and accompaniment of one another. This enactment of transformation arises in virtue of our recognizing, in such a "seeing," the mutuality of otherness in which all creation—including ourselves—stands in virtue of the graced contingency of its radical dependence. I will argue that this transformative seeing good is what renders our vulnerability as an "epiphanic" locus in which the contingency of radical dependence invites us into the enactment of the grace of mutual welcome and accompaniment that provides room for us to be "guests to one another" in and for a fractured world.

2 See Charles Taylor, *Sources of the Self: The Making of the Modern Identity* (Cambridge, MA: Harvard University Press, 1989), 245–47, for Taylor's trenchant analysis of the displacement of grace in the wake of the "rationalized Christianity" that gets intellectually distilled into various forms of Deism.

AUTONOMY RECONSIDERED:
HUMAN MUTUALITY AS LOCUS FOR MORAL FREEDOM

I have already noted that key elements for the account of human freedom I am presenting will be drawn from an interpretation of Immanuel Kant's treatment of human freedom as it is exercised in the workings of our moral agency. Central to this interpretation will be resituating the concept of "autonomy," which is fundamental to Kant's understanding of moral freedom, as an exercise of human finite reason *as it is situated in human mutuality*. In contrast to what has been, until recently, the prevailing account of Kantian moral autonomy, one that is consonant with the atomistic construals of human identity and agency woven into the immanent frame, I will be arguing that autonomy is more appropriately understood differently, as structured and functioning within the context of the human mutuality that forms the matrix in which human moral agency is exercised. My argument will be offered on both conceptual and historical/textual grounds that indicate that a social construal of autonomy is more adequate with respect both to the moral character of the freedom that it functions to mark out and to the overall account that Kant himself gives of the structure and the finality of human moral agency.[3] I will be arguing that the human mutuality that provides the context for autonomy is constituted by the reciprocal connections of respect within which each moral agent is called to stand in relation to other human agents as a member of what Kant terms a "kingdom of ends" or an "ethical commonwealth." I will then argue that a central feature of the mutual respect in which agents stand in constitutive moral relation to one another is a coordinate recognition of the fragility of the finite human freedom

3 I have presented a more extensive account of how Kant's discussion of the human freedom exercised in the practical (moral) use of reason is fully embedded in human social relationality in *The Social Authority of Reason: Kant's Critique, Radical Evil, and the Destiny of Humankind* (2005). The major addition to that account that is made here connects such recognition of mutuality, as it is embedded in moral autonomy, to a corresponding recognition of human vulnerability as also a constitutive element of that mutuality.

that constitutes our moral agency. This mutual recognition of the fragility of our freedom, moreover, will then provide one vantage point from which we are enabled to discern our vulnerability as a locus for receptivity to the working of grace.

According to what I earlier termed an immanentist reading of Kant, one that is consonant with the naturalist and atomist presuppositions of the immanent frame, the human freedom exercised in the practical use of reason is construed in terms of choices made by individual moral agents abstractly conceived: They stand unaffected by their relations to other human beings in whatever society of which they may be part.[4] Such agents make decisions as abstract members of a timeless "intelligible world" standing, at best, in a formal relation with an equally abstract set of fellow members of that world. In characterizing the moral exercise of reason as autonomous—that is, as self-legislating—Kant certainly highlights the fact that responsibility for the appropriate moral exercise of reason rests squarely in the hands of individual moral agents. This emphasis on agential responsibility in his discussion lends some persuasive weight to an immanentist reading that construes autonomy in individualist terms. At the same time, however, the immanentist reading tends to take little notice of the social presuppositions deeply embedded in Kant's account of moral agency in terms of the *mutual* accountability that agential self-governance entails for shaping and directing one's conduct.

One instance of this inattention to the social dimension of autonomous agency can be found by considering how Kant's articulation of autonomy as an expression of such mutual accountability is placed within the context of the distinctive focus

4 John Rawls's device in *A Theory of Justice* (Cambridge, MA: Belknap Press of Harvard University Press, 1971) of the "veil of ignorance" (136–42) in which he places the contracting parties of the "original position" is a notable attempt both to take account of the standard abstract rendering of the autonomy of individuals and to temper its abstractness by allowing knowledge of some limited features of human relationality to enter into the contractual deliberations that, significantly, are to articulate principles for governing freedom in its *societal* exercise.

on the reflexivity that Charles Taylor identifies as fundamental to modernity's construal of subjects and selves. Within this context, Kant's articulation of autonomy can be understood as reconfiguring and expanding the scope of agential accountability as it has been understood in the principles of the "common morality"[5] he seeks to undergird critically. Agents are now explicitly and reflexively accountable for the *normativity* of their moral judgments as well as for the conduct such normativity governs. Such agential accountability for normativity, however, does not thereby render that normativity, nor the autonomy that is accountable to it, as "subjective," "private," or "individualist" in the manner that many immanentist readings of Kant would often have it. Kant's own seminal treatment of autonomy that puts self-governance at center stage of discussions of moral agency is instructive on this point. In the *Groundwork of the Metaphysics of Morals* he explicitly presents his account of moral self-governance as nothing more than a more precise articulation of a principle that every agent already grasps, as a matter of practical apprehension, in acting morally.[6] This principle bears upon the manner in which the exercise of moral agency carries within its very form a commitment to order one's actions to unconditioned good—that is, to that good which requires, under penalty of rendering one's agency practically unintelligible, unconditional recognition by all rational agents.[7]

5 For the significance of the "common morality" in Kant's work, see Alan Donagan, *The Theory of Morality* (Chicago: University of Chicago Press, 1977), 4–9; this classic study explores commonalities in the moral theories of Aquinas and Kant.

6 Immanuel Kant, *Groundwork of the Metaphysics of Morals* (G), in *Practical Philosophy*, trans. and ed. Mary J. Gregor, *The Cambridge Edition of the Works of Immanuel Kant* (Cambridge: Cambridge University Press, 1996), 58–59; in AA, the standard German edition, this passage is found at AA 4:403–4. In this regard, the thrust of his argument is not principally against theoretical moral skepticism but against practical self-exemptions from the moral order that we are inclined to enact for our own benefit.

7 See, for instance, Stephen Engstrom, *The Form of Practical Knowledge: A Study of the Categorical Imperative* (Cambridge, MA: Harvard University Press, 2009), 124–27, 155–59, 167–78.

This indicates that one important way in which Kant affirms the social character of the context of intelligibility within which his account of moral agency functions is through his insistence on the universal character of the normativity for which moral agents take responsibility in the exercise of their autonomy. Universality helps to mark out the *shared* moral space—the "kingdom of ends"—that constitutes the field in which all members of the moral community of autonomous agents hold themselves mutually accountable, to themselves and to one another, in the exercise of their moral freedom. In accord with this principle of universality, the fundamental manner in which one violates the standard of mutual accountability that it enunciates is to make an exception for oneself: This standard holds for everyone, except for me. This preference for "the dear self" is the concrete manifestation taken by the "inversion of maxims" that Kant sees at the root of the "radical evil" that is the primary form of self-corruption and self-incapacitation of human moral agency.[8]

In a similar way, a further element is prominent in the overall linguistic and conceptual structure of Kant's account of the workings of human moral agency. This further element—the language of "law" and "legislation" that he frequently uses to characterize the structure of moral principles and the way in which agents take responsibility for their enactment—also manifests the social embeddedness of Kant's account of agency. It draws its intelligibility, not from some private dynamic of self-enclosed inner self, but from public, social, and institutional contexts that form the primary locus of its conceptual articulation as "law."

The final consideration that I will propose in favor of reading Kant's account of autonomy as situated within the matrix of human social relationality emerges from a social focus and orientation that is fundamental not merely to his understanding of autonomy but to the critical enterprise as a whole. Given the centrality of human freedom, construed as autonomy, to Kant's

---

8 See *Religion within the Boundaries of Mere Reason*, Part I, III, "The Human Being Is by Nature Evil," R AA 6:32–39/Cam 79–85.

critical philosophy, this coordinate repositioning of his entire philosophical project into a social mode should not be surprising.[9] For at least the last three decades, an emerging stream of Kant interpretation has taken note of the social, cultural, and political trajectories that Kant imparts both explicitly and implicitly to his critical project. These trajectories can be traced both within what are considered the "major" critical texts and in the various essays that were published on a range of topics throughout the 1780s and 1790s.[10]

For my purposes, two related elements in Kant's work that have been noted in this stream of interpretation will be of help for, first, discerning the social dimensions of Kant's account of autonomy and, second, exploring the import this has for a theological articulation of the loci open to the workings of grace in the fractured conditions of secularity's immanent frame. One element is the extent to which this social reading of the critical enterprise indicates that it is driven by an anthropological question:

9 Kant underscores the centrality of freedom for the entire critical project in the "preface" to the *Critique of Practical Reason*: "Now the concept of freedom, insofar as its reality is proved by an apodictic law of practical reason, constitutes the *keystone* of the whole structure of a system of pure reason, even of speculative reason" (CprR AA 5:3–4/Cam 139; emphasis in original).

10 A notable precursor for this line of interpretation is Lucien Goldmann, *Immanuel Kant* (London: New Left Books [Verso], 1971), a translation from the French *La communauté humaine et l'univers chez Kant* (Paris: Presses Universitaires de France, 1948), and German *Mensch, Gemeinschaft und Welt in der Philosophie Immanuel Kants* (Zurich: Europa Verlag, 1945). Some other Kant commentators who have later articulated this social dimension include Sharon Anderson Gold, Allen Wood, Pauline Kleingeld, Roger Sullivan, Jeanine Grenberg, Robert Louden, Philip J. Rossi, Howard Williams, and Holly Wilson. An argument might also be made that this recent attention to the significance of social dimensions of Kant's work might be considered a retrieval or revival of some of the interpretive and philosophical concerns that informed the work of some of late nineteenth- and early twentieth-century neo-Kantians; see, for instance, David N. Myers, "Herman Cohen and the Quest for Protestant Judaism," *Leo Baeck Institute Yearbook* 46, no. 1 (2001): 195–214; Thomas E. Willey, *Back to Kant: The Revival of Kantianism in German Social and Historical Thought, 1860–1914* (Detroit: Wayne State University Press, 1978).

What role does humanity, as a species that is both embodied in the spatio-temporal workings of nature and endowed with the moral freedom to which they hold one another accountable, play within the workings of the cosmos as the locus for both theoretical and moral intelligibility?[11] The other element is the extent to which Kant articulates that role specifically in terms of what he takes to be humanity's moral vocation. This vocation consists in being agents for establishing and maintaining a cosmopolitanism world order in which the exercise of human freedom bears not only upon each agent's individual moral destiny but also upon bringing about, as the social outcome of human history and culture, the "highest good" for humanity as a species. Let me explicate each of these in turn before moving on to a discussion of how the recognition of mutuality that this social reading of Kant's critical project sees embedded in the exercise of moral autonomy also encompasses a recognition of human vulnerability as one of the constitutive elements of that mutuality.

On this social reading of Kant's project, the fundamental anthropological question "What is humanity?" that drives his critical philosophy is framed in view of both the immense dignity and the deep fragility of the relations in which humanity stands before the workings of the cosmos. Perhaps the most well-known expression of this concomitant awareness of our human dignity

11 Kant signals the importance of "the human" in a gloss he later makes (in the Jaësche *Logic*) that expands into four the three well-known questions he poses in the "Canon of Pure Reason" in the *Critique of Pure Reason* (CPR A805/B833) as encapsulating the project of "critique": "The field of philosophy in this cosmopolitan sense can be brought down to the following questions:
1. What can I know?
2. What ought I to do?
3. What may I hope?
4. What is man [humanity]?
Metaphysics answers the first question, morals the second, religion the third, and anthropology the fourth. Fundamentally, however, we could reckon all of this as anthropology, because the first three questions relate to the last one" (JL 9:25). *Jäsche Logic*, AA 9:1–150; Cam: *Lectures on Logic*, 519–640.

and our human fragility as we stand before the cosmos is the passage from the *Critique of Practical Reason* cited in the last chapter in which "the starry skies above" and "the moral law within" are two objects Kant considers appropriate for evoking a response of awe from our finite human freedom. Kant situates the mutuality of our human freedom—or, alternately, the reciprocity of our autonomy—as fully engaged with the contingency of the cosmos, which presents itself to us as the world of "what is," even as that mutuality also marks the locus in which we are enabled to engage that world morally by enacting in it "what ought to be." Awareness of the reciprocal connections of the freely offered respect within which one stands to all other human agents—in Kant's terms, awareness of one's membership in a "kingdom of ends"—thus also brings with it a deep sense of the fragility of our finite freedom. The recalcitrance of the world "as it is," manifest in the workings of the contingency of uncertain outcome impinging upon our human vulnerability, remains obdurate even in the face of the recognition that we are called to stand with one another in mutuality in our engagement with it.

The second element that figures prominently in a social reading of Kant's critical project is the "cosmopolitan perspective" that delimits what I will term the worldly and historical scope of humanity's moral vocation. A cosmopolitan perspective enables agents to envision and to work for the establishment of conditions under which human freedom can function both individually and socially as a counterweight to the dynamics of the "radical evil" of obdurate self-preference as it interweaves itself into the workings of contingency. Such obdurate self-preference manifests itself socially in the competitive emulation Kant terms "unsocial sociability," an emulation that, as it functions in the context of human social, economic, and political institutions, all too often escalates into the conflicts in which radical evil takes its most destructive form: war. Cosmopolitanism thus serves as what I term "a social anthropology of hope."[12] This provides a horizon

12 For war as the social form of radical evil, see Philip J. Rossi, "War: The

for action within which agents may envision the moral character of their human interaction and relations as indexed not just to their "unsocial sociability" and the conflict it fosters but also to an emergent community of enacted reciprocity that arises from a recognition of the mutuality of freedom and gives a distinctive social shape to the moral vocation of our embodied human finite agency. This hope, as Kant concretely articulates it, is that human beings see themselves as empowered to work together to fashion a world order for enduring peace. For Kant, the locus from which human freedom most fully shapes the social conditions of human agency lies in its capacities both to envision and to work for the establishment of what, in *Religion within the Bounds of Mere Reason*, he terms "the ethical commonwealth": an enduring social linkage of agents that provides humanity with its most potent counterweight to the social obduracy of human self-preference. It is not without significance, moreover, that Kant also identifies the ethical commonwealth with the ideal form and dynamic of "the Church."[13]

The two elements I have just described—the anthropological thrust of the entire critical project and the cosmopolitan perspective that provides hope for the achievement of humanity's moral vocation in the world—thus suggest a further dimension to a social construal of autonomy. This dimension is especially pertinent to the project of articulating an anthropology of situated

Social Form of Radical Evil," *Kant und die Berliner Aufklärung: Akten des IX. Internationalen Kant-Kongresses*, ed. Volker Gerhardt, Rolf-Peter Horstmann and Ralph Schumacher (Berlin: Walter de Gruyter, 2001), Bd. 4:248–56. For radical evil as the obduracy of self-preference and its connection to "unsocial sociability," see Philip J. Rossi, "Cosmopolitanism: Kant's Social Anthropology of Hope," in *Kant und die Philosophie in weltbürgerlicher Absicht: Akten des XI. Kant-Kongresses 2010*, ed. Stefano Bacin, Alfredo Ferrarin, Claudio La Rocca, Margit Ruffing (Berlin: Walter de Gruyter, 2013), Bd. 4:827–37.

13 See Philip J. Rossi, *The Ethical Commonwealth in History: Peace-Making as the Moral Vocation of Humanity* (Cambridge: Cambridge University Press, 2019), for a more extensive discussion of the relationship between the ethical commonwealth and the church.

freedom that offers space for discerning the workings of grace from within the immanent frame. This dimension is constituted by the fact that human relationality, which provides the context for the exercise of moral autonomy, is deeply embedded in the contingencies of the cosmos and of our human fragility. Kant's anthropology inscribes our human freedom, our human mutuality, and the working out of our common moral vocation into the embodied conditions of our spatio-temporal finitude and thereby inscribes them into the conditions of our common human vulnerability as part of the cosmos. The human power for bringing about good thoroughly pertains to, and is rooted in, a finite practical reason, a moral agency that, as it is exercised in a world of contingency and of human sociality, recognizes that its capacity for bringing about good, though fragmentary and fragile, is also empowered in hope by bonds of human mutuality as well as by the embodied relationality that embeds humanity in the cosmos.

Such fragmentary and fragile character is not simply an outcome arising from the limited scope of the good we each have power to effect; it also arises to the extent that the endurance of much of the good that we each actually effect requires that others also do what is needed to bring it about and to sustain it. The mutuality that we recognize as offering hope that together we can effect the good that "ought to be" also participates fully in the fragility of our human finite freedom. Insofar as we each stand alone in the face of the impingements of contingency, our finitude provides thin and tenuous protection to our core dignity of spirit. Under these conditions, human power for bringing about good—rooted in the fragmentary, fragile exercise of finite reason—stands on the slender and precarious footing of a social relationality that is both embedded in cosmic contingency and subject to the dynamics of our obdurate self-preference and unsocial sociability. Human fragility stands aware that, in this world of contingency, it cannot of itself, either individually or communally, fully guarantee enduring stability for an order of what "ought to be," the order that fully accords with the dignity and the fragility of our human embodied spirit.[14] Yet the absence of such a guarantee with respect to our own powers—as Kant presciently saw—is precisely a condition for the hope that empowers us to sustain our own commitment and our commitment to one another in the particular enactments that constitute living out our part of our common moral vocation.[15]

When this inscription of human autonomy into the fragility of our embodiment into the contingency of the cosmos is put in terms of Neiman's depiction of our human condition as located within "a metaphysic of permanent rupture,"[16] it opens the possibility for seeing how the recognition of the mutuality of our freedom is also a recognition of the mutuality of our embodied vulnerability. The freedom that is exercised in view of the relationality that renders it morally intelligible is what enables us to pay proper "attention to the pieces" that constitute the fractured landscape of our human condition in an age of secularity. Freedom is exercised here from coordinates upon which the trajectories of human mutuality and human vulnerability converge to frame a horizon of hope that makes it possible to envision how we can be participants with one another in the healing of fracture. I will propose in the next section that one central way to bring about such healing is by enacting the challenging hospitality

14 See Philip J. Rossi, "The Crooked Wood of Human History: The Ethical Commonwealth and the Persistence of Evil," in *Nature and Freedom/Natur und Freiheit /Nature et Liberté; Proceedings of the XII International Kant Congress*, ed. Violetta L. Waibel, Margit Ruffing, David Wagner (Berlin: Walter de Gruyter, 2018), Bd. 4:2591–98.

15 Neiman comments: "Instead of knowledge of the future, God gave us hope. Kant turned this thought into one of his greater arguments: if we knew that God existed, freedom and virtue would disappear. It's an act of Providence that the nature of Providence will forever remain uncertain.... Our very skepticism is a providential gift. What binds the real and the rational together must be so fragile that it will seem miraculous—and on occasion the miracle occurs. As with any other miracle, it takes something like faith to perceive it." Susan Neiman, *Evil in Modern Thought: An Alternative History of Philosophy* (Princeton: Princeton University Press, 2002), 327.

16 Neiman, *Evil in Modern Thought*, 80.

of welcoming the depths of the vulnerability and otherness embedded in our relationality to one another, the hospitality through which, in Steiner's striking phrase, we learn to be "guests to one another on this crowded, polluted planet."[17]

GRACE, VULNERABILITY,
AND THE INFLECTIONS OF CONTINGENCY

In the course of the previous chapters I have often indicated that our human vulnerabilities and the contingencies that bear upon them stand in a tensive relationship to the atomist and naturalist coordinates for construing human identity and agency that function within the dominant social imaginary of modernity. On the one hand, our vulnerabilities are seen to be deeply ingredient in the dynamics of the fractured circumstances in which humanity finds itself situated in the cultures of secularity. They stand as an unyielding marker of the persistent finitude circumscribing our human situation, a finitude that is allowed no recourse beyond the naturalistic limits of the immanent frame for the healing of fracture. On the other hand, the deepest fractures that impinge upon our vulnerabilities often exhibit persistent recalcitrance even in the face of the ministrations of instrumental reason, which is taken as the one effective mode for remedy and redress of the damage that follows in the wake of the impingements of contingency. Yet, for the deepest of fractures— lives cut short in infancy and youth, in life projects gone amiss, in the ravages of pain and suffering inflicted by human neglect, violence, or enmity, and in disastrous consequences ensuing from even the best of our intentions—restoration and healing, if they come at all, rarely do so without scars that inscribe themselves deeply in memory and can persistently mark subsequent trajectories of individual and shared experience. This inscription of fracture into memory and history is one index of the extent to

17 George Steiner quoted in Theo Hobson, "On Being a Perfect Guest: The Tablet Interview: George Steiner," *The Tablet* 259 (August 13, 2005): 15.

which the disenchantment of workings of the world, including those workings shaped by human agency, makes the metaphysical import of history starkly manifest: History provides coordinates within which human freedom and the workings of contingency give the human world its metaphysical structure of fracture and its trajectories of incompleteness.

Modernity's disenchantment of the world has helped to exhibit the deep connection between metaphysics and history that is embedded in our fractured human circumstances; yet this connection remains stubbornly opaque to the instrumental reason to which modernity has assigned the task of dealing with the consequences of that fracture. Awareness of this incapacity of instrumental reason with respect to the deepest manifestations of human fracture and vulnerability predates both its character-istic modern valorization and the attention that modernity has given to the depth to which fracture can persist in the histories ingredient in our personal and social identities. The Book of Job, that ancient and enduring marker of how our embodied human vulnerability can be fractured by the contingency of uncertain outcome, takes note of this incapacity. Underlying Job's defense that the woes besetting him are unwarranted is an awareness that he—and indeed all humans—dwells in a dissonant space in which instrumental efforts to fend off the inequitable workings of contingency in the world are all finally futile when measured against the depth of human moral expectation. Clarity about the indifference of the world to human hopes and purposes renders the very existence of that world morally pointless. The case Job makes against the smugness of his friends' claims that blameless suffering is not part of the contingency in a world is not simply a defense of *his* innocence within that world. It is also a *protest* that puts the immanent order of the world itself at issue by rendering morally problematic, not simply the particular workings of the world's contingency afflicting him, but the world's very being.

It thus may not be too anachronistic to suggest that the Book of Job had already plotted out key coordinates of the deep moral fault line that now has become manifest in our human engagement with the disenchanted world that is central to the formative social imaginary of secularity. The workings of such a world, which in principle is devoid of any inner moral purposes, cannot but present a blank and indifferent face to any human demand for justice, to any hope of definitive fulfillment of core human aspirations. Job himself sees far more clearly than his friends that contingencies in a world that simply runs its own course, standing indifferently to human hopes and purposes, do not order themselves according to justice unfailingly rendered to humans who dwell in that world. Job is well aware that he is not the only, nor likely the last, righteous one who has been subject to what is, humanly speaking, unwarranted suffering but which, for "the world in which human purposes are enmeshed," is merely another indifferent outcome.

A reader attuned to Job's acute sensitivity to the fragility of a human life led righteously in a contingent world may very well wonder at the end, when his fortunes have been "restored," whether the echoes of all that has befallen him can—or, more pointedly, even *should*—ever fully fade from his memory, from our memory, or from the memory of the God Job has called to account. Job's new progeny open new space in his world for human satisfaction, yet they cannot refill the space made abruptly empty by the calamity that befell his other children. That past is stubbornly recalcitrant to full erasure, so even the renewal of Job's prosperity and well-being does not suffice to exhibit the cosmos as working in ways that are normatively fully intelligible to the deepest aspirations of our enfleshed vulnerability.

The haunting, dramatic expression the Book of Job gives to the depths of human vulnerability in the face of the contingency of the world exposes the incapacity of instrumental reason to engage those depths to the satisfaction of our hopes that justice be manifest in the workings the world. That same incapacity is central for the analyses of the moral constrictions and contradictions consequent upon the disenchantment of the world that

Taylor, Neiman, and Steiner offer. They provide accounts of that incapacity that transpose the tensions laid bare in the Book of Job into a range of contemporary philosophical inflections that indicate how those tensions are particularly consequential for efforts to understand what it is to be human in the circumstances of secularity. They each help to point out key conceptual and moral pressures that arise from this tension as it plays itself out in a secular culture that, in order to be consistent with its naturalistic presuppositions, does not even allow us, like Job, to call God to account.

According to their accounts, the immanent frame has helped to bring the contingencies that bear upon our enfleshed human vulnerability into a new and challenging critical focus: A fundamental condition of our humanity in a disenchanted world is that humanity stands alone in its vulnerability, aided neither by nature nor by grace, before the random encroachments of a contingency blindly indifferent to our human purposes. A disenchanted world not only leaves our vulnerabilities bereft of any protection from the impingements of contingency, save those we can devise on the basis of our instrumental reason; it also fails to provide any measure adequate for weighing the moral significance of those vulnerabilities, particularly when contingency presses hard upon them. Neiman appositely remarks: "It would be easy to acknowledge that not controlling the natural world is part of being human, were it not for the fact that *things go wrong*. The thought that the rift between reason and nature is neither error nor punishment but the fault line along which the universe is structured can be a source of perfect terror."[18] Yet even as our enfleshed vulnerability in the face of the workings of contingency can be acknowledged as fundamental to the disenchanted circumstances of our humanity in the cultures of secularity, it nonetheless stands as a condition that is also fiercely contested in multiple ways with regard to its own import (if any!) for the

18 Neiman, *Evil in Modern Thought*, 80–81.

immanent frame. Our vulnerability is contested with respect to its moral and metaphysical significance; it is contested with respect to the framing of appropriate responses to its individual and social manifestations; and it is contested with respect to the bearing these all then have upon our self-understanding and the relations we have to one another—and all of this in a world in which contingency itself constitutes the common space in which we dwell in vulnerability with one another.[19] Inasmuch as our human vulnerabilities stake out key coordinates for the finitude with which we are encompassed in the immanent frame, these contestations indicate that whatever sense we can give to our vulnerability, to our condition of finitude, will be central for shaping the self-understanding that is constitutive for an anthropology of situated human freedom. Put simply, our humanity is deeply configured in and by our vulnerabilities.

In the context of the central role that instrumental reason has been accorded by the immanent frame for shaping our response to the workings of a disenchanted world, gaining control of the workings of the world emerges as a core strategy for protecting our vulnerabilities against the ravages of things gone wrong in the spaces of worldly contingency. Implicit in this strategy is a construal of our finitude that indexes it to the measure of control we can gain over the contingent circumstances of our lives. Yet, as both Taylor and Neiman point out, much of the testimony of the human history that has unfolded in the wake of increasing human instrumental capacity to direct and alter the working of the world to human purposes seems to belie the promise instrumental reason holds out for overcoming the contingencies that

19 See Charles Taylor, *A Secular Age* (Cambridge, MA: Belknap Press of Harvard University Press, 2007), 684: "But then the question may arise whether any humanistic view, just because it is woven around a picture of the potential greatness of human beings doesn't tempt us to neglect the failures, the blackguards, the useless, the dying, those on the way out, in brief those who negate the promise. Perhaps only God, and to some extent those who connect themselves to God, can love human beings when they are totally abject."

heedlessly impinge upon our vulnerabilities. Our efforts to ward off the workings of contingency all too often bring in their wake further impingements, unforeseen and unplanned, that are of at least as much consequence as the ones we originally hoped to ward off.[20]

Such unintended consequences have become increasingly evident, for instance, with respect to human efforts to use more and more of the finite material resources of our planet without due attention to the longer-term consequences for local, regional, and even planetary ecosystems. The economic benefits they yield are beginning to become manifest as relatively short term and limited once they are measured against the deep systemic disruptions to the biosphere that eventually follow in their wake. From efforts to harness the power of atomic energy for peaceful as well as destructive purposes, to gaining knowledge and control of the dynamics of life at the most elemental genetic level, to the processing of information at speeds and levels of complexity once thought unimaginable, the larger the scope of human control has apparently become, the greater the challenge has become of comprehending—let alone properly governing—the consequences, intended and unintended, that have ensued upon our efforts to control and master the impingements of contingency.

The increasingly urgent and complex global ecological crisis thus serves as a looming, ever more insistent marker of the inherent incapacity of instrumental reason to function regulatively—that is, to offer definitive and reliable normative coordinates for engaging our vulnerabilities that will enable us, from within the limits of our finitude, to make our fractured human circumstances more fully accord with the world as it "ought to be." The challenge to the adequacy of instrumental reason here, moreover, is compounded by the need to enlarge the scope of our engagement with vulnerability so that, beyond

20 See Neiman, *Evil in Modern Thought*, 73–75. She notes that, with respect to the workings of contingency, "small dreams are no surer to become true than great ones, and either can become nightmare in the blink of an eye" (74).

our human vulnerabilities, it also encompasses the vulnerabilities in play within the interrelated workings of the biosphere, locally, regionally, and globally. The moral opacity that confronts instrumental reason in dealing with the mutuality embedded in our human vulnerabilities is thus further thickened by a nexus of interrelatedness that requires us to locate our human vulnerabilities within a planetary life system that human activity is placing under unprecedented pressure. Such an account of the full scope of mutuality in which our human freedom is situated would thus require that it also be located within this larger context of interrelated planetary life and the systems that function to sustain it.

For the purposes of this effort to provide an anthropology of situated human freedom that enables discernment of the workings of grace in a culture of secularity, however, developing a full account of its location within a larger pattern of planetary interrelatedness belongs to a later—and likely much larger—stage of the project. The more immediate and pressing task is to engage the opacity that impedes the cultures of secularity from *fully attending to the moral structure of mutuality that is embedded in our human vulnerability.* That structure stands particularly opaque for a culture of secularity in view of the naturalist and atomistic strictures the immanent frame places on the scope of our moral understanding, so making the moral import of that structure manifest will be crucial for effecting any enlargement of the moral horizon of the immanent frame. In order to do this, we can usefully turn to another locus of contestation within the immanent frame about the significance of our human vulnerabilities, one that the immanent frame has in fact recognized as having a bearing upon the core moral structure of our human mutuality.

This other locus of contestation is the immanent frame's placement of "rights" as the central social modality for protecting some of our core human vulnerabilities when they come under threat. Taylor leaves little doubt that the articulation of the discourse of rights and the development of institutional structures and practices to enhance and protect them has been a major moral achievement of modernity. Yet he also argues that the secular discourse of rights, particularly when its protective function is framed merely through a procedural syntax that avoids substantive claims about what constitutes the human, has too often proved a clumsy instrument for protecting our most fundamental human vulnerabilities as they are affected by the contingencies both of the workings of nature and of the vagaries of human intentionality and action in history: "In public debates standards that are unprecedentedly stringent are put forward in respect of these norms and are not openly challenged. We are meant to be concerned for the life and well-being of all humans on the face of the earth ... we subscribe to universal declarations of rights. ... But it is a quite different thing to be moved by a strong sense that human beings are eminently *worth* helping or of treating with justice, a sense of their dignity or value."[21]

Such discourse is limited precisely by its incapacity to articulate from within the naturalistic and atomistic presuppositions of the immanent frame an understanding of what it is to be human substantive enough to enable us to recognize and respect human worth and dignity in all our fellow humans—including, most pointedly, "the failures, the blackguards, the useless, the dying, those on the way out, in brief those who negate the promise [of human greatness]."[22] Taylor maintains that the instrumental and procedural uses of reason are inadequate to undergird an account of human worth and dignity sufficient to empower fully the mutual acknowledgment of our human vulnerability that is necessary for an adequate recognition of the value of the persons who bear those rights. On his account, the procedural basis for rights that the immanent frame is constrained to offer on the basis of its naturalistic presuppositions fails to provide a robust moral understanding of the constitutive relationality in which we stand to one another as persons. Just as instrumental reason fails to provide a regulative principle that is sufficient to provide a

21 Taylor, *Sources of the Self*, 515.

22 Taylor, *A Secular Age*, 684.

robust normative horizon to constrain heedless exploitation of the natural world, a procedural understanding of rights is inadequate to articulate how our human relationality inscribes a normativity into our vulnerability that requires us to respond in timely, appropriate, and effective ways to serious impingements upon the vulnerability of others. In contrast, Pope Francis, in his message for the 2014 World Day of Peace, "Fraternity, The Foundation and Pathway to Peace," provides a particularly apposite substantive characterization of the normativity inscribed into human relationality that escapes such procedural understanding: "In the heart of every man and woman is the desire for a full life, including that irrepressible longing for fraternity which draws us to fellowship with others and enables us to see them not as enemies or rivals, but as brothers and sisters to be accepted and embraced."[23]

In sum, the contingencies of the world thus often manifest our vulnerabilities in ways—such as severe lifetime physical disabilities or affective incapacities, social circumstances foreclosing possibilities for even minimal development of basic human capacities for knowledge and well-being, large and small dislocations of people in consequence of war, civil unrest, economic instability, or natural disaster—that stretch to and beyond the limit of the capacity of the chief moral sources that the immanent frame recognizes, justice and benevolence, to move us to respond in timely, appropriate, and effective ways to those affected by them. Taylor notes the doubly ironic consequences that have followed in the wake of modernity's construal of these moral sources as the "hypergoods"[24] that trump all others in

23 Pope Francis, "Fraternity, The Foundation and Pathway to Peace," Message for World Day of Peace, January 1, 2014, §1. See also Francis's more recent encyclical letter, *Fratelli tutti* (October 3, 2020), which provides extensive discussion, in terms of concepts of solidarity and fraternity, of the fundamental importance of the inclusive recognition of human mutuality we require of one another.

24 Taylor, *Sources of the Self*, 63: "Hypergoods" are "goods that are not only incomparably more important than others but provide the standpoint from which these must be weighed, judged and decided about."

efforts to fend off the ravages of contingency. There are, on the one hand, the consequences that follow upon the working of a paradox that is embedded in these hypergoods: "[the] higher the morality, the more vicious the hatred and hence the destruction we can, indeed must wreak."[25] However noble the ideals these hypergoods have inspired, they have also had enormous power to distort, dominate, and crush: "The Kharkov famine and the Killing Fields were perpetrated by atheists in an attempt to realize the most lofty ideals of human perfection."[26]

Taylor's account echoes Foucault's insight into the irony that "the ways in which high ethical and spiritual ideas are often interwoven with exclusions and relations of domination."[27] In the absence of the recognition that we are linked in mutuality through our shared human condition of vulnerability, as Nietzsche and Dostoyevsky both recognized, benevolence and compassion all too readily become masks for a contemptuous pity. On the other hand, however, there are other consequences (noted earlier in chapter 3) that, arising from an awareness of the distorting and destructive power of hypergoods, lead us to settle for a moral "realism" in which "it's safer to have small goals, not too great expectations, be somewhat cynical about human potentiality from the start."[28] This double irony, which captures much of the core moral tension at work in the immanent frame's construal of our humanity, seems to confront us with the uncomfortable choice between "various kinds of spiritual lobotomy and self-inflicted wounds."[29]

Taylor's criticism that the immanent frame offers an unpalatable choice between being morally crushed by the power of impossibly lofty ideals and retreating into a moral "realism" that is a self-induced stifling of our highest moral aspirations resonates with some of the bleaker accounts that postmodernism

25 Taylor, *A Secular Age*, 709.

26 Taylor, *Sources of the Self*, 518–19.

27 Taylor, *Sources of the Self*, 518.

28 Taylor, *A Secular Age*, 699.

29 Taylor, *Sources of the Self*, 520.

gives of its predecessor culture. It stands here, however, as also framing an important positive coordinate for this effort to render the discourse of grace intelligible for a culture shaped by the immanent frame. Taylor's criticism helps to diagnose the source of the incapacity of the immanent frame to engage fully the finitude that is deeply inscribed in our human vulnerability: The naturalist and atomist presuppositions of the immanent frame render it—and us!—inattentive to the way in which our vulnerability, in all its finitude, provides nonetheless an inescapable fundamental marker of our mutuality. "Is the naturalist affirmation [of benevolence] conditional on a vision of human nature in the fullness of its health and strength? Does it move us to extend our help to the irremediably broken, such as the mentally handicapped, those dying without dignity, fetuses with genetic defects?"[30] Taylor's pointed question here can be usefully connected to a point that Neiman makes to characterize one highly influential strand, paradigmatically articulated by Hegel, at work in the totalizing dynamic of the immanent frame. She quotes from *The Introduction to the Lectures on the Philosophy of World History*: "The sole aim of philosophical inquiry is *to eliminate the contingent*."[31] From the perspective of instrumental reason, what more effective way is there to eliminate the contingent than to attempt to render us invulnerable to its workings and thereby to overcome the very finitude that is fundamental to our being human?

Taylor suggests that what is needed to move beyond the dilemma that hypergoods pose to the naturalism of the immanent frame is not resignation to the conclusion "that the highest spiritual aspirations must lead to mutilation or destruction" (or, as he puts it more concretely, that we have to choose "between various kinds of spiritual lobotomy and self-inflicted wounds").[32] What is instead needed is a transformative seeing that alters how we see, value, and respond to our human condition of vulner-

---

30 Taylor, *Sources of the Self*, 517.

31 Cited in Neiman, *Evil in Modern Thought*, 89, emphasis in original.

32 Taylor, *Sources of the Self*, 520–21.

ability as it manifests how deeply our mutuality is embedded in the fractured interplay of contingency. This mode of seeing involves "a transformation of our stance towards the world whereby our vision of it is changed."[33] On Taylor's account there is a "double-sidedness" to such a transformative seeing: Both the one seeing and what is seen are mutually implicated in the transformation effected in the "seeing." Acknowledgment of the possibility of such mutual transformation, he argues, is not peculiarly modern—a point of particular significance for my argument in that the lineage of this modern dynamic of transformation can be traced back to earlier understandings of the working of grace: "In fact, the notion of a transformation of our stance towards the world whereby our vision of it is changed has traditionally been connected with the notion of grace."[34]

What I am thus proposing is that possibilities for discerning the working of grace in the spaces of worldly contingency can be opened up by a transformative engagement with the immanent frame *in the very loci it considers least likely to manifest grace.* These are the very human vulnerabilities that mark human finitude as an unavoidable yet destabilizing vector in the moral dynamics of the immanent frame. At issue here is the measure of the meaning and significance of the human in the face of the contingencies that manifest, often enough in devastating and deeply destructive ways, how fully our vulnerability shows us immersed in a finitude that poses a threat to all meaning. The naturalism of the immanent frame, moreover, has raised the ante for what is at stake: From its perspective, there is (and was) no God to hold accountable for the finitude that is manifest in our vulnerabilities and in the contingencies that impinge upon them. As Neiman has noted, in an account of the disenchantment of the natural that resonates with Taylor's, the human vulnerabilities that have become painfully evident in a world in which the inner workings of nature are devoid of purpose and stand indifferent,

33 Taylor, *Sources of the Self*, 449.

34 Taylor, *Sources of the Self*, 449.

at best, to human well-being now mark a major point of moral fracture within and for the intellectual culture of modernity: "To open any door of the world to contingency is to open the whole to chaos; if law isn't universal, it isn't really law. To accept that the world we inhabit is not the best is to accept essential unintelligibility that leaves understanding in the dark."[35]

Within the context of the moral fracture that ensues upon resistance to our human condition of finitude, Neiman's trope of "homeless" exhibits even greater moral poignancy. The homeless condition in which we stand on the fractured landscape of modernity is not merely the outcome of the workings of a contingency that is heedless of our human purposes; *it is at least as much a result of our inattention to one another*. We do not merely stand homeless; we stand homeless as strangers to one another— and, often enough, as strangers to ourselves—a condition that is pointedly captured in a trope that has become one of the most characteristic of postmodern sensibility: otherness. Grappling with the multidimensional reality of "otherness" opens possibilities with power to expose the depth and the breadth of our individual and systemic failures to enact the one condition that will provide us with a genuine home on the fractured landscape of the immanent frame: the reciprocity of mutual welcome in hospitality by which we accept one another in our full mutual vulnerability.

Instead of such mutual welcome, however, the conditions of living with one another that we have helped shape (sometimes actively, sometimes by acquiescence) in civic life, in the marketplace, in the dynamics of religion and of culture, which should be ones conducive to the flourishing of all, have all too often been ones we have misshaped (as much by inattention as by ill-intent) to one another's detriment. At the outset of the twenty-first century, the dynamics of so many interactions within our dominant sociocultural, political, and economic structures provide scant evidence from which to glean firm assurance that we, as a species, have yet learned how to make the space on which

35 Neiman, *Evil in Modern Thought*, 93.

we dwell a fitting "home" for one another as fellow humans, let alone for other living beings with whom we share the earth. Our hesitation to welcome, our refusals to welcome, arise from what Neiman has so incisively described as the precariousness of our own sense of "being at home" in a world shot through with contingency. We thus seem to provide to one another, in the social worlds we construct to affirm "our" identity over against "theirs," little to suggest that we have mastered the skills to share, in a modicum of peace, even a small space side by side with fellow human beings who are not the "us" delimited in our parochialisms. Inscribed deep in our failures, great and small, to welcome the displaced, the uprooted, the homeless, as well as in the license we often give ourselves to drive strangers away with coldness, hostility, and even violence, is a refusal to recognize that we, too, stand "homeless" in our human condition and that, as George Steiner pointedly remarks, all of us "are guests of life on this crowded polluted planet."[36] Unsure of how welcome we truly are in the world, even when we stand in a privileged place, our welcome for others falters, lest opening the door to them bring with it contingencies that might displace us as well.

The next chapter will thus articulate what is required to engage the immanent frame in its resistance to seeing how the good of mutuality that is embedded in our human vulnerability empowers a mutually transformative hospitality that extends to the full depth of the otherness in which we stand to one another. I will be arguing that central to such a transformative seeing is the recognition of the radical dependence that is nothing less than the enacted hospitality from which the otherness that constitutes creation in all its variety and fullness has been graciously brought to be and is sustained in and by the abundant, indeed by the inexhaustible, all-embracing goodness of God.

36 Theo Hobson, "On Being a Perfect Guest: The Tablet Interview: George Steiner," *The Tablet* 259 (August 13, 2005): 14.

Part III

Shaping a World of Grace

Chapter 6

Vulnerability, Mutuality, and the Transformative Grace of Otherness

GRACE AS TRINITARIAN HOSPITALITY: SEEING THE GOOD OF OTHERNESS

THE OPENING CHAPTER TOOK NOTE of Taylor's suggestion that the "articulation of anthropologies of situated freedom" could offer "breathing space" for the human spirit as it dwells within the fractured landscapes of value, truth, and meaning that seem to constitute vast swaths of the aftermath of late modernity. Upon such broken terrain, the human spirit often finds its expansive yearnings constricted under a stifling atmosphere generated by the self-enclosed and self-enclosing dynamics of the cultures of secular modernity, particularly in the forms that Taylor designates as "exclusive humanism" and the various "anti-humanisms" that often have then been its spawn. Such a spiritually enervating atmosphere has, according to Taylor, fostered a moral blindness, all too often self-inflicted, to the "constitutive goods" that, by providing the deepest moral sources formative of our human self-identity, would make genuine human flourishing possible even upon the fractured terrain of secularity.

The subsequent chapters then proposed two related lines of exploration along which to articulate an anthropology of situated freedom that is appropriate for the circumstances of the cultures of secular modernity. The first line of exploration both charted key lines of fracture traversing the terrain of secularity and marked the workings of the constricting currents generated from the "social imaginary" that provides exclusive humanism with an "immanent frame" for its horizons of meaning and value. What emerged along this line of exploration was a "conceptual topography" that converges upon two fundamental markers for locating the elements of human situatedness in a time of secularity. One of these markers is human finitude, inscribed both in the mutuality of our freedom and in the vulnerability in we stand before the face of otherness; the other is the twofold contingency, the contingency of absolute dependence that marks the abundant gratuity of creation, and the contingency of uncertain outcome that both encompasses our finitude and provides the space of otherness for the interplay in history of our human freedom, mutuality, and vulnerability.

These markers, finitude and contingency, then offered a basis from which to take up the second line of exploration; this exploration focused upon identifying and articulating, within the human interplay of freedom, mutuality, and vulnerability in the space of contingency and otherness, an appropriate anthropological vantage point from which to discern the workings of the divine activity of all-encompassing goodness that Christian theology and practice have named "grace." The key marker that emerged along this line of exploration was the good of human mutuality, particularly as it is most powerfully inscribed in the welcoming recognition of our shared human vulnerability that is enacted in hospitality: Human freedom, enacted in hospitality as the acknowledgment of our situatedness in mutual human vulnerability, finds itself "graced" in and by this call to recognize in such vulnerability the transformative power of the otherness that is now encountered and embraced in welcome.

Inscribed in this enactment of freedom as the recognition of our human vulnerability that renders us mutually open to the welcoming of otherness is a vantage point offering a perspective that runs athwart the self-enclosed explanatory dynamics of excusive humanism. That framework takes its bearings from the deep and often deadly impingements upon our vulnerabilities that the workings of contingency inflict upon humanity as it dwells on the fractured terrain of modernity and its aftermath. From the vantage point of exclusive humanism, such impingements and the deep fractures from which they arise cannot but decisively count against the workings of whatever might be indicative (as grace is taken to be) of a transcendent presence enabling human flourishing. From that perspective, moreover, it is only the elimination of contingency and of the vulnerability it threatens that would be sufficient to provide conditions for human flourishing—whatever the cost such invulnerability might exact from the lives and well-being of those unfortunate to be caught in the maws of the instrumental reason that needs to be enlisted in the production of those conditions.

In contrast, the marker constituted by the recognition that a welcoming freedom provides for the mutuality inscribed in our human vulnerability offers a different vantage point from which to view the impingements of contingency upon our shared vulnerability in a time of secularity. This vantage point is framed by the reciprocity of mutual enactments of welcome by which we fully accept one another both in our mutual vulnerability and in the otherness that constitutes us in our difference to one another. *In hospitality, our human mutuality freely embraces and enfolds the otherness and the difference that are the very marks of the abundant gratuity of creation.*

It is thus from the vantage point provided by hospitality that this final chapter returns to Taylor's suggestion about the importance of articulating anthropologies of situated freedom for the secular times in which we dwell. I take his suggestion to indicate that careful attention to the character of our human freedom—precisely as it is situated in the mutual interplay of contingency, vulnerability, and mutuality—provides a marker from which it becomes possible to discern, even from within the various mists and miasmas of that loom upon the terrain of secularity, persistent

modalities that invite us to participate in present and future enactments of grace. Within the interplay of these factors of our human
situatedness, hospitality functions as *the transforming and transformative recognition of otherness and difference*. It serves as a
central locus for the discernment of transformative grace as it is
enacted whenever, in the mutuality of human freedom, otherness
is acknowledged, welcomed, and fully embraced.

In theological terms, a hospitality that is attentive to our mutual
human vulnerabilities and to the otherness that constitutes us in
difference to one another thereby renders us open to a radically
transformative "seeing good" that, within the context of our situated
human freedom, is empowered by the graciousness of God's hospitality in its Triune inflection. On the account I am proposing,
divine hospitality is enacted as a Triune outpouring of abundant
life-bestowing welcome within which the distinctive working of
each Person expresses a corresponding manner of "seeing good" in
its empowerment of grace. It thus is operative as the following:

- the "seeing good" that enacts creation as the space of
  otherness in which all that is contingent comes to be;[1]
- the "seeing good" that enacts the Incarnation as the
  human enfleshment of the Word by which the divine
  transformatively takes into itself the brokenness of
  humanity and of the entire world; and
- the "seeing good" that pledges eschatological completion
  through the working of the Spirit enlivening, renewing, and
  elevating humanity and the cosmos of which we are part.

In concert, these inflections of a divine "seeing good" are what
make it possible for the concrete exercise of our situated human
freedom to enact a graced reciprocity of welcoming by which we

---

1 To appropriate a phrase used by David Burrell, this could be termed
creation as "original grace." See David B. Burrell, "Creation as Original
Grace," in *God, Grace and Creation*, ed. Philip J. Rossi (Maryknoll, NY:
Orbis, 2010), esp. 103–6.

fully accept one another in mutual vulnerability and otherness. In such reciprocity lie the possibilities for our situated freedom to turn even the fractured ground presented by the immanent frame of secularity into a place of graced and gracious welcome for the good of all that is other. To use George Steiner's striking phase, in enacting such hospitality—especially in the circumstances of "this crowded, polluted planet"—our situated freedom teaches us "to be guests to one another."[2] Understood in these terms, the Triune manner of divine hospitality provides a basis for articulating at least three counterpart inflections for our concrete human enactments of our hospitality that, in contrast to the self-enclosure of the "social imaginary" of secularity, make possible (indeed insistently make possible!) the discernment of the presence and working of grace on the fractured landscape of secularity:

+ The grace of hospitality *enacted as transforming vision*: This enables us to see good "all the way down" throughout our human mutuality, our human vulnerability, and the multiple ways that we all are mutually entwined in the good of the cosmos in all its contingency.

In the language of the tradition of the spirituality of St. Ignatius of Loyola, the enactment of this inflection of the transforming grace of hospitality may be articulated as seeking and finding God "in all things"—including (and perhaps especially) in all the contingency and contingencies of the world. It might also be expressed as a dictum that nothing—including the stubborn historical residue of all enactments of evil—stands outside the transformative activity of grace. In this regard, it is of significance that Taylor associates the transformative power of "seeing good" with "a central idea of the Christian tradition, that people are transformed by being loved by God, a love that they mediate

2 Theo Hobson, "On Being a Perfect Guest: The Tablet Interview: George Steiner," *The Tablet* (August 13, 2015): 14.

to one another."[3] He further elaborates on the significance of this transformative seeing by framing it in terms of the ways such vision is enacted in Dostoevsky's "healing figures" such as Zosima and Alyosha: "What will transform us is an ability to love the world and ourselves, to see it as good despite the wrong. But this will only come if we can accept being part of it, and this means accepting responsibility."[4]

Taylor notes further that in Dostoevsky's portrayal the empowerment of such an ability to love is not explicable in terms of a self-sufficient immanence: "Loving the world and ourselves is in a sense a miracle, in the face of all the evil that it and we contain.... Involved in this [miracle] is our acceptance of love from others."[5] In consequence, recognition of the vulnerability that goes "all the way down" in the humanity of all of us may be discerned as a locus within which our authentic selfhood, especially as it stands in human mutuality, may be rendered open to the transforming presence of the grace that is an enactment of divine love:

♦   This is the grace of hospitality *enacted as mutually transformative*: This enables us to welcome the human otherness we encounter in one another and the otherness of the cosmos not as threatening hostility but as a difference that invites the incarnate empowerment of a kenotic "unselfing" that affirms all that is.[6]

This mutually transformative enactment of hospitality is inscribed in many narratives from the world's religious traditions

---

3 Charles Taylor, *Sources of the Self: The Making of the Modern Identity* (Cambridge, MA: Harvard University Press, 1989), 452.

4 Taylor, *Sources of the Self*, 452.

5 Taylor, *Sources of the Self*, 452.

6 H. Richard Niebuhr describes this in terms of a dynamic of reconciling trust that culminates in the replacement of an "ethics of death" by an "ethics of life." *The Responsible Self: An Essay in Christian Moral Philosophy* (New York: Harper & Row, 1963), 135–44.

that engage the dynamics and consequences of welcoming—and of failure to welcome—the other, the stranger. The Lucan parable of the Good Samaritan may be the most familiar of the narratives from the gospels that provide a perspective upon the workings of human hospitality from the vantage point of the ever-offered enactment of God's all-encompassing hospitality. Luke, moreover, provides an illuminating counterpoint on the mutually transformative power of hospitality by the very setting in which he depicts Jesus telling another parable of hospitality: the Great Feast (Luke 14:15–24 RSV). This parable immediately follows a description of the enacted dynamics of guest and host in the home of the Pharisee who has invited Jesus to dine, upon which Jesus then provides parabolic commentary (Luke 14:7–14 RSV); that commentary pointedly runs counter both to the enacted self-privileging of the guests in their choosing "the place of honor" (v. 7) and to the self-interest and self-regard that Jesus discerns in the host's offering invitations only to those in a position to "invite . . . in return" (v. 12).

In consequence, the subsequent telling of the parable of the Great Feast opens, both in its setting and its telling, an even more expansive possibility for an enacted hospitality that, in view of an awareness of our mutual human vulnerability, is transformatively different from what host and guests alike displayed at the home of the Pharisee. This transformed hospitality now issues, not only from a generosity that sets aside all consideration of (mutual) recompense and that, in both its offering and reception, pays no mind to status, but from an expansive inclusiveness that goes out to "the highways and the hedges" (v. 23) in *active search* to bring in those at the margins.[7] The enactment of hospitality Luke proposes for the hearers of the parable to envision follows the lineaments of movement that—both with respect to its putting

---

7 For a more extended treatment of this point, see Philip J. Rossi, SJ, "Sojourners, Guests, and Strangers: The Church as Enactment of the Hospitality of God," *Questions liturgiques—Liturgical Questions* 90, nos. 2–3 (2009): 121–31.

aside considerations of status and recompense and its engagement "all the way down" to the least and to the forgotten—resonates with the kenotic pattern set forth in the Pauline hymn of Philippians 2:5–11:

♦   The grace of hospitality *enacted as bringing wholeness in and for the world*: It rescues, cherishes, and brings to fullness all the pieces of a fractured world.

This third inflection of "seeing good" is appropriately aligned with the enlivening, renewing, and elevating work of the Spirit in history in and through a community in which welcoming and accompaniment enact healing solidarity. It is a seeing good that makes it possible for our concrete enactments of human freedom to have the capacity to turn even the fractured ground presented by the immanent frame of secularity into a place of graced and gracious welcome for the good of all that is other. In this manner of seeing good, and in the hospitality that it empowers, the Spirit of the incarnate and now risen God makes possible not merely individual acts of healing welcome. The Spirit also forms and constantly enlivens a new community, which provides a space of welcome that encompasses all, and empowers respite and healing especially for those whom the principalities and powers of the world turn away in indifference and hostility. In this inflection of seeing good, no matter how unwelcoming the face of the world's contingency and in spite of human collusion with that hostility by practices of exclusion, human freedom still can be rendered open to being constitutive of a community in which all are welcome, no matter how shattered their and our human circumstances have become. Seeing good in the manner of God's inclusively welcoming Spirit enables us to envision a gathering of humanity into a community of full mutuality, one in which wholeness takes shape in virtue of the recognition and reverencing of our shared vulnerability.[8]

8 Flannery O'Connor's short story "Revelation" offers a fictional narrative

A crucial element in this gathering together of community, in consequence, will be the attention we give to picking up and including the "fragments"—the broken lives that have been shattered and tossed aside by the impingements of contingency and human hostility—in our shaping, with and for one another, a human wholeness for which we are all called to be participant with and for one another in its attainment. As Susan Neiman has trenchantly observed about the circumstances of our age, given the modality and scale of the evil that humans have inflicted on one another and upon our world in recent centuries, "Wherever so many structures of modern thought have been shattered, whatever sense we find must be incomplete. *Attention to the pieces is now all the more important.*"[9]

As I will propose in the next section, Neiman's comment suggests that an important element in the gathering of humanity into a community of full mutuality can also be articulated as a "seeing good" that bears upon the manner in which we can be enabled to participate in the enactment of human wholeness in and for a world in which human brokenness is manifest in many forms. This attentive seeing good of the "fragments" consists in a capacity for our envisioning concrete possibilities for healing engagement, piece by piece, large and small, with the consequences of "the historical persistence of evil": the scars and wounds, the twists and turns, the traumas, the fractures, and the rubble that stubbornly persist in the social reality that lies athwart our embodied human vulnerability.

This is the seeing good, moreover, that Pope Francis has proposed and articulated in his exhortations that we should work together to enact "a culture of mercy": a culture that empowers hope for human healing and wholeness amid secularity's landscape

---

that displays the delightfully ironic inclusivity of divine hospitality. *Flannery O'Connor: Collected Works* (New York: The Library of America, 1988), 633–54.

9 Susan Neiman, *Evil in Modern Thought: An Alternative History of Philosophy* (Princeton: Princeton University Press, 2002), 326.

of fractured meanings and values. It is a culture "based on the rediscovery of encounter with others, a culture in which no one looks at another with indifference or turns away from the suffering of our brothers and sisters."[10] By envisioning, encouraging, and enabling practices and enactments of healing, reconciliation, and hospitality upon the terrain of secularity, a culture of mercy accords an enlivening welcome to human vulnerability and otherness in all its variety and radical contingency. In Pope Francis's vision, the fruit of this welcoming and healing embrace of humanity's present and past fracture will come to its fullness in a future order of enduring peace among peoples: "Only thus will it be possible to build societies that are open and welcoming towards foreigners and at the same time internally secure and at peace."[11]

ENACTING A CULTURE OF MERCY ON THE FRACTURED TERRAIN OF SECULARITY: GRACE AS ACCOMPANIMENT OF OTHERNESS

As we enter the third decade of the twenty-first century, we find our human freedom to be situated in a self-enclosed social imaginary that has brought in its wake a pluralizing fracturing of meaning and value, accompanied by intensification in the frequency, scale, and destructive consequences of human social conflict. From the vantage point of an immanentizing secularity, this pluralizing fracture is often construed as reason for recognizing, be it in resignation, defiance, or indifference, that the world stands "on its own," void of transcendence, as well as of anything that might be construed as an inherent purpose, let

10 Pope Francis, Apostolic Letter *Misericordia et Misera* (November 20, 2016), §18.

11 Pope Francis, "Address to the Diplomatic Corps," January 9, 2017; see also *Misericordia et Misera*, §20: "Mercy impels us to roll up our sleeves and set about restoring dignity to millions of people; they are our brothers and sisters *who, with us, are called to build a 'city which is reliable'*" (emphasis mine).

alone one favorable to human well-being.[12] Within this secular situatedness of both self-enclosure and fracture, the three inflections of seeing good sketched in the previous section are especially fraught with significance, all the more so in view of the dynamic of human divisiveness that has taken particularly virulent forms in the global culture of the early twenty-first century. Since the self-enclosed and self-enclosing dynamics of the cultures of secular modernity do not provide a vantage point that allows a concern for human good and purposes to be a part of the world's own inner workings, they can only permit us to conclude that the world most assuredly is *not* made for our welcome. To this indifference of nature, moreover, we all too often find ourselves, individually and communally, adding the human patterns of unwelcome that lend credence to Hobbes's classic depiction of deadly competitive combat as the fundamental baseline of human social interaction: *bellum omnium contra omnes*.

The outcome of this pernicious confluence of nature's indifference and human hostility is that the conditions of human life at the outset of the twenty-first century have provided little from which we may glean firm assurance that we have yet learned how to make the space on which we dwell a fitting "home" for one another as fellow humans, let alone for other living beings with whom we share the earth. We find ourselves situated in a world in which neither the workings of nature nor the social, political, or economic worlds we construct to affirm and protect "our" identity over against "their" identity provide guarantee that we have mastered the skills to share, in a modicum of peace, even some little space side by side with those we perceive as, not our human brothers and sisters with we whom can utter "we," but instead as "others" who, if they are to be regarded at all, can be recognized only as "them." This has perhaps been most poignantly

---

12 Neiman has incisively pointed out the consequences: "Science may have abolished the sense that the world is inhabited by forces with wills of their own, and in this way reduced the *unheimlich*. But the price is enormous, for all of nature stands condemned. Human beings themselves become walking indictments of creation" (*Evil in Modern Thought*, 236–37).

manifest in recent decades in the phenomena of extensive human displacement that has rendered homeless and unwelcome far too many of our fellow humans, be it on a massive scale of abrupt uprooting induced by war and violence, or in incremental patterns of displacement and migration fueled by economic, cultural, social, and now environmental dislocations.

Human inhospitality is by no means a new phenomenon, nor is ungrateful and grasping behavior on the part of those to whom hospitality has been extended. It is thus no accident that a grim paradigm of human hostility, the story of Cain and Abel, occurs early in the narrative that, for Jewish and Christian communities of faith, is constitutive of their relation to the One who lovingly welcomed humanity into being and whom they name God.[13] The ruptured relation between the siblings Cain and Abel ensues upon the grasping inhospitality by which their parents, Adam and Eve, ruptured the intimate relationship of enlivening companionship they had with the "LORD God [who walked] in the garden in the cool of the day" (Genesis 3:8 RSV). In this context, Cain's invitation to his brother, "Let us go out to the field" (Genesis 4:8 RSV), is a chilling inversion of the divine hospitality of creation by which God welcomed humanity into the cosmos: It is the first, but by no means the last, time that fraternal companionship is transmuted to a walk unto a brutal death.

My reference to the Cain and Abel story at this point, however, is not simply to provide a reminder that inhospitality, long before the emergence of the cultures of secularity, has been a significant locus in which we rebuff and violate rather than reverence and respect our common human vulnerabilities or turn otherness into enmity. I offer this scriptural story, instead, as a point of entry from which to indicate how "seeing good," as the threefold inflection of enacted hospitality, bears directly upon concrete possibilities for discerning grace within a time of secularity and upon its terrain of fractured meaning and value

13 A parallel narrative about the first two sons of Adam, Habil (Abel) and Qabil (Cain) is found in the Qu'ran (5: 27ff.).

that situates the exercise of our human freedom. This story, to the extent that it continues as a thread of *our* human story even in a time of secularity, provides one important point of reference from which to articulate a situated anthropology.[14] I am thus proposing, *contra* the grim image of conflict that Hobbes provides of our human "state of nature" and its primal narrative instantiation in Cain's murder of Abel, that these modes of enacted hospitality can play a significant role in making possible, in and for a time of secularity, a transformative, life-affirming inversion of the deadly inversion of hospitality displayed in the fratricidal tale of Cain and Abel even as its long shadow extends over our age. This enlivening inversion is into what Pope Francis calls a "culture of mercy," a culture that displays, in and though mercy enacted in multiple forms, the working of grace.

As noted earlier, the Pope characterizes this culture as "based on the rediscovery of encounter with others, culture in which no one looks at another with indifference or turns away from the suffering of our brothers and sisters."[15] Central to such a culture of mercy is a transformative seeing of otherness, one that enables us to enact, for and with one another, the profound good of a hospitality in which, be it as hosts or as guests, our vulnerability, our mutuality, and our otherness find full acknowledgement and welcome. In theological terms, such "seeing good" is empowered by the recognition of *the good of the fundamental otherness in which all creation stands in virtue of the graced contingency of its radical dependence.* This radical dependence is nothing less than the enacted hospitality from which the otherness that constitutes

---

14 As Jonathan Sacks points out, the sibling rivalry that provoking Cain's violence against Abel "may be natural but it is not inevitable." In fact, on the account Sacks gives of the series of four Genesis narratives of sibling rivalry, of which the murder of Abel by Cain is the first and the reconciliation of Joseph and his brothers is the last, it is a feature of the human condition that can be overcome "by generosity of spirit, [and] active efforts of reconciliation" *Not in God's Name: Confronting Religious Violence* (New York: Schocken Books, 2015), 170.

15 Apostolic Letter, *Misericordia et Misera* (2016), §20.

Creation in all its variety and fullness has been graciously brought to be and is sustained in and by the inexhaustible goodness of God. It is that by which the otherness and the difference we name "creation" originally comes to be and is sustained as a place of welcome. Our human acknowledgement of this radical dependence thus renders the vulnerability in which we stand precisely as "other" to one another into an "epiphanic" locus for the enactment of grace to and for one another: In recognizing our mutual otherness, precisely in virtue of our shared contingency of radical dependence, we are invited into enactments of that grace of mutual welcome that provides room for us to be "guests to one another" in and for a fractured world. Such enactments of welcome, moreover, find completion in being gathered together into practices of accompaniment through which we are enabled, by being with one another, to be participant in bringing into being the work of Emmanuel: The "God with us" in whose Incarnation the divine transformatively and unfailingly accompanies us in history by taking into itself the vulnerability and brokenness of humanity and of the entire world.

Such enactments of grace, in hospitality and accompaniment, stand counter to the workings of exclusion, hostility, and violence that from the vantage point of the self-enclosed explanatory dynamics of excusive humanism seem deeply encoded in our human make-up. In a world that stands blankly indifferent to human aspirations and rife with what I have earlier termed the "contingency of uncertain outcome," it can be both theoretically and practically daunting to see these destructive phenomena as anything but unavoidable outcomes of the social dynamics of competition that, as the base condition for humanity's survival, provides an exiguous (at best) platform for its flourishing.[16] In contrast to this, I have been proposing an account of the situatedness of our human freedom within which we are invited to a

16 Hobbes, as noted above, starkly described these dynamics as an on-going state of war; Kant, more perceptively in my judgment, termed them "unsocial sociability."

"seeing good" of the fundamental otherness in which all creation, including our humanity, stands—*an otherness that is good precisely in virtue of the freely enacted contingency of its radical dependence*. In consequence, it becomes possible to discern and to affirm our mutual vulnerability, mutuality, and otherness as the loci in which and from which we are offered "grace" as *those possibilities that empower us to enact, in hospitality and accompaniment with one another, the overcoming of fracture and of that which brings fracture about.*

"Grace" may thus be discerned as creating a space of possibilities for us to act, even as we ourselves are fractured, in ways that help one another in the work of healing the fractures of the world.[17] In that space, it becomes possible for us both to become "guests to one another" in hospitality and then to accompany one another in full mutual recognition of the shared fragility that marks our human finitude. Practices of welcoming, hospitality, and accompaniment thus provide signal instances for such shared enactments of grace; they emerge and are shaped in response to the invitational space opened by the contingencies that insistently call upon us, fractured as we all are, to find ways to dwell in peace with one another across the range of the particular fractured times, places, and events in which we encounter one another in this time of secularity.

CODA:
TOWARD A THEOLOGICAL ANTHROPOLOGY
OF ACCOMPANIMENT AND PEACE

As noted in the opening chapter, Taylor's project to articulate a philosophical anthropology focuses on the centrality of reflective self-interpretation for addressing questions of what it

---

17 On this point, the Jewish notion of *tikkun olan* (repairing the world) provides a significant point of reference. See Elliot N. Dorff, *The Way Into Tikkun Olam (Repairing the World)* (Woodstock, VT: Jewish Lights Publishing, 2005).

is and what it means to be human.[18] In *Sources of the Self* and *A Secular Age* he provides extensive accounts of the emergence and the workings the socio-cultural context in which human efforts at reflective self-interpretation are now situated: This is the "immanent frame" of meaning and value that provides the self-enclosed "social imaginary" for a secular age. At the core of what he diagnoses as the central spiritual malaise of secular cultures emergent from the West have been the ways in which the workings of the immanent frame have fostered and promoted modes of narrowed self-understanding and self-interpretation, chief among these is the "buffered self": A self that is "disengaged" and that "sees itself as invulnerable, as master of the meanings of things for it."[19]

Such shrinking of the horizons for our self-understanding is of consequence not merely for the theoretical articulations of what it is and what it means to be human that function in the academic and intellectual quarters of the cultures of secularity. On Taylor's account, such constricted self-understanding is also of consequence for framing the possibilities for how all of us will manage to continue living with one another within the limits of our planetary home. A time of secularity finds us living in a world in which, despite growing awareness of damaging cumulative impact that human activities, even ones undertaken with benevolent intentions, can and do have upon the very conditions for the well-being and flourishing of all life on Earth. In addition, we have devised precious few institutions for effectively controlling, let alone curtailing or eliminating, the dynamics of the many forms of individual and communal conflict by which we inflict

18 See "Self-Interpreting Animals," *Human Agency and Language: Philosophical Papers I* (Cambridge: Cambridge University Press, 1985), 45–76, for an early articulation of the importance of self-interpretation for Taylor's anthropological project.

19 Charles Taylor, "Buffered and Porous Selves," *The Immanent Frame* (Social Science Research Council blog), September 2, 2008, https://tif.ssrc.org/2008/09/02/buffered-and-porous-selves/.

deadly violence on one another, nor for curbing the production and distribution of the weapons and technologies of indiscriminate destruction.

As I will indicate below, Taylor's account points us in a direction that frames a horizon from which to envision possibilities for living in concord with one another that address the urgent (and related) challenges of planetary fragility and human divisiveness. This horizon is framed by articulating the situatedness of our human freedom in terms of the recognition of the shared vulnerability of our finitude. It is such recognition, I have been arguing, that invites us to an inclusive welcoming of otherness, a welcoming we enact precisely as we situate that otherness within a horizon constituted by our participation in the "seeing good" that concretely enacts in and for the world the threefold manner of divine hospitality. As noted earlier, the possibilities envisioned for human encounter and interaction within this horizon run counter to the presumption, embedded in the atomic individualism of the immanent frame, of the inevitability of a deadly Hobbesian dynamic of conflict in shaping our dealings with one another. Rather than being bound to a condition of endless human conflict, this horizon enables us to envision with and for one another those enactments of hospitality and practices of accompaniment for and with "the other" that provide conditions for our living together in concord.

Taylor's account thus points out that the anthropologies implicit in the immanent frame have allowed us to distract and even to blind ourselves to the dimension of our reflective self-interpretation that is most fundamental to the constitution of what and who we are as human. This dimension is the finitude that both situates our freedom, vulnerability, and otherness within the space of mutuality and is also a mark of the contingency of radical dependence in which we stand as part of a creation we had no role in bringing about. In view of our radical dependence, our human finitude is constituted as the locus for those fields of meaning, encounter, and interaction in which, in

Steiner's pointed phrase, we are invited to become "guests to one another." It is thus within this space of finitude that we are each constituted in our humanity and for one another as enfleshed spirit: as receptively oriented, in and through our finite activities in a finite world, to a transcendent order that, in its enactments of grace in the Triune inflection of hospitality, anticipates the offer and bestowal of "fullness" exceeding the measure of our finite human expectations.[20]

Taylor's discussion, in *Sources of the Self*, of the "seeing good" that enacts the good that it sees is an important locus in which he delimits the coordinates for the spaces of human finitude that, in his philosophical anthropology, serve as loci in which the presence and working of what theology terms "grace" may be discerned.[21] These spaces are opened in and by our recognition of the vulnerability that goes "all the down" in the finite humanity of us all. In such recognition, our authentic selfhood is rendered open to the transforming presence of the grace that in theological terms is nothing other than divine love itself—a point that Taylor reminds us has been given abidingly powerful expression both in the Johannine writings and in the novels of Dostoevsky. By referencing this point, Taylor's account helps us to identify our human vulnerability and the space of mutuality it creates as a primary locus for the possibility of our participation in enactments of

20 Such receptive orientation to the offer and bestowal of fullness is a point on which one could locate a convergence between Taylor's account and Karl Rahner's notion of a "supernatural existential" regarding how humans stand with respect to the gratuity with which God enacts grace. For a useful account of Rahner's notion as it was formed in the context of the mid-twentieth-century dispute about the distinction between nature and grace and about the "natural desire for the beatific vision," see David Coffey, "The Whole Rahner on the Supernatural Existential," *Theological Studies* 65, no. 1 (2004): 95–118.

21 Taylor, *Sources of the Self*, 448–55; see Philip J. Rossi, "Seeing Good in a World of Suffering: Incarnation as God's Transforming Vision," In *Godhead Here in Hiding: Incarnation and the History of Human Suffering*, Bibliotheca Ephemeridum Theologicarum Lovaniensium 234, ed. Terrence Merrigan and Frederik Glorieux (Leuven: Peeters, 2012): 453–66.

grace: Grace is enacted in and through our welcoming and our accompaniment of one another in ways that are abundantly inclusive in their attentiveness to the deepest and most fragile points of our human vulnerability.

In consequence, seeing the good of the mutuality that is embedded in our human vulnerability empowers a mutually transformative hospitality that extends welcome to the full depth of the otherness in which we stand to one another. As an appropriate complement to such hospitality, this "seeing good" further empowers us to fashion practices of accompaniment with those welcomed in hospitality. These practices comprise various modes of making possible a "being with" that sustains the enactment of our being "guests to one another": *Accompaniment becomes the sustained mutual enactment of hospitality*. Accompaniment opens space and provides the time for encompassing together any and all—friend or stranger, ally or enemy—we encounter "on life's way," however like us they may be, or however unlike and "other" they may be. Fully interwoven into such accompaniment, moreover, is the dynamic of a "time-full" sustaining of hospitality that draws us into partnership and conversation those into whose company the contingencies of the world have drawn us.[22] In such partnership and conversation, the inclusiveness of sustained hospitality calls for attending to the voices of all whom we "companion"—and most especially and intently to the barely audible whisperings and to the very silences of those who seem voiceless among those in whose company and with whose otherness we have been graced to be. Framed in terms of the inclusive Triune manner of hospitality, practices of accompaniment

22 See Niebuhr, *The Responsible Self*, 91–97, for a discussion of the "time-full self," of which an important element is the self's "compresence" with what is not oneself. For a suggestive sketch of some of the important modalities of accompaniment, see Tomáš Halík, "Recognizing the Signs of the Times," in *Renewing the Church in a Secular Age: Holistic Dialogue and Kenotic Vision,* ed. Charles Taylor, José Casanova, George F. McLean, João J. Vila-Chã, Cultural Heritage and Contemporary Change, Series VIII: Christian Philosophical Studies 21 (Washington, DC: The Council for Research in Values and Philosophy, 2016), 147–55.

provide a horizon of hope in and through time for enacting human wholeness amid the pervasive plurality of meanings and values that mark the cultures of secularity.

As loci for enactments of grace that complement hospitality by sustaining a dynamic of "being with," practices of accompaniment also draw our attention to ways in which secularity's dynamic of plurality provides an invitation to discern grace from a horizon in which it is enacted *within and for the very multiplicity* of the immanent frame. In this, practices of accompaniment also stand athwart one of the influential ways in which the immanent frame of secularity has construed itself as closing off by its very multiplicity possibilities for enactments of grace. To the extent that modernity and the secularity that is its offspring have brought in their wake a pluralizing fracturing and fragilization of meaning and value, this has been construed as powerful reason for taking a stance of resignation to humanity's inevitable enclosure within a world void of transcendence. In contrast, the Triune inflection of the seeing good that, in the context of our finitude, vulnerability, and otherness, enacts hospitality and accompaniment in a world of fractured multiplicity suggests otherwise: The explosive multiplicity we encounter in our time of secularity invites us to engage our fractured world, not from a horizon of resignation to its fragmentation, nor from a horizon of nostalgia for past dynamics of hegemonies of meaning, but from a horizon of hope in *graced multiplicity*, one that is framed in reference to the encompassing hospitality of God in which we, amid and for the multiplicity of the world, are invited and challenged to participate. It is grace enacted by attending in respectful and even joyful welcome to each, every, and all the pieces of a fractured world.

This horizon of graced multiplicity has come into view, at least in part, through the fissures and differences that, in the aftermath of modernity, we now can see more clearly at work in the human cultures in which we articulate our self-understanding and exercise our freedom. This horizon enables us to discern, even in the context Taylor terms the "galloping pluralism" of the nova effect, enlarged possibilities for intensifying and expanding our capacity for enacting, in ways attentive to the grace offered in multiplicity, appropriate forms of wholeness for our humanity and for our world.[23] This horizon of grace in multiplicity provides significant conceptual and imaginative resources for a renewed understanding of the workings of divine and human interaction in the fragility of an enfleshed human finitude located in the multiple contingencies of both creation and human history. These resources offer a basis for understanding and appreciating both the varied and incomplete character of the human receptivity into which God seeks entry in grace, and the richly plural operative modality of the grace with which God, in this time of secularity, appropriately nurtures that receptivity along paths to human fullness.

In a time of secularity, we inhabit a human world in which many fields of meaning and practice that formerly have been delimited as well-bounded spaces for dwelling in secure possession of our identities, be they ethnic, linguistic, religious, or cultural, have increasingly become open and unstable. This instability has provided circumstances in which recognizing our finitude and vulnerability, exercising our freedom in full mutuality, enacting hospitality, and sustaining it in practices of accompaniment are fraught with great risk, even as they also are charged with radically transformative power. The risk arises from the potential that the destabilizing multiplicity of "otherness" has to expose the depth and the breadth of our individual and systemic resistance to what—and who—we perceive as standing unlike us, apart from us, encroaching on "our" spaces, and thus provides a challenge to the boundaries of our own identity. Embedded in this risk is the potentiality for letting fear and resistance to otherness and the instability of multiplicity set us upon a Hobbesian trajectory that renders us all permanently hostile strangers to one another.

At the same time, there is a profoundly transformative power that can issue precisely from our encountering, from the expansive horizon of "seeing good," the destabilizing multiplicity

23 Charles Taylor, *A Secular Age* (Cambridge, MA: Belknap Press of Harvard University Press, 2007), 299–300.

of otherness and broken meaning. From this horizon, the very multiplicity that engenders fear and resistance can be transformed by seeing its good precisely as a marker and reminder of *how deeply our own identities are themselves embedded in the otherness in which and from which we delimit ourselves*: The mutuality that shapes out identity in freedom is itself a mutuality of and in otherness. Seeing the good of otherness and multiplicity as (surprisingly) already part of who we are enables us to discern the extent to which our identities are already shaped by dynamics in which the "other" already stands within the ambit of our identity: Our identity and agency is thus constituted within an "immanent otherness" that has its roots in our very sociality and mutuality as human.[24] The explosive multiplicity of the immanent frame invites us to engage our fractured world from a horizon oriented from the seeing good that is the encompassing hospitality of God, a horizon that enables us to discern, even in the "galloping pluralism" of the nova effect, enlarged possibilities for intensifying and expanding our capacity for enacting wholeness for our humanity and for our world. Within this horizon, recognition of our own immanent otherness then provides a particularly pointed reminder of an element fundamental to the realization of such human flour- ishing and wholeness: the project of working with one another to envision and enact ways that, in the midst of all the otherness we communally and individually bring with us, enable us to dwell in concord with one another across the contingencies of time upon the finite and fragile planet entrusted to us. In a time of secularity, in a world of multiplicity of otherness and of broken meaning, the Triune inflection in which we are invited to "see good" provides the locus for the enactment and discernment of grace by calling

24 Recognition that we are, in a profound sense, the very one whom we have "othered" has functioned as a *locus classicus* in paradigmatic tales of moral recognition. One powerful instance: The prophet Nathan's confron- tation of King David, in which David's anger at the rich man who appro- priated the poor man's lamb is turned into David's own self-recognition of his adultery with Bathsheba once Nathan says "You are the man!" (2 Samuel 12:1–7 NAB).

upon us in freedom to build, by inclusive hospitality and faithful accompaniment, an enduring culture of mercy and peace.

What bearing, then, does such a project of building a culture of mercy and peacemaking have for what was set out as the task of this work—namely, articulation of an anthropology of situated freedom appropriate to the circumstances of the cultures of secular modernity? Implicit in this question is the possibility that how we exercise our freedom with and for one another may play a role—perhaps a crucial role—in reshaping the very contours of our situatedness. In this case, an anthropology of situated freedom that is closely attentive to the circumstances of the cultures of secular modernity may be one that enables us most appropriately to engage and to heal the most pervasive fracture of our secular situatedness: the exclusivities and divisiveness that have become infectiously rife throughout our human social interaction, particularly those exclusivities and divisions out of which come the most violent and virulent forms of social conflict.[25] Those divisions manifest a dynamic that reenforces the self-enclosure of the immanent frame, one that seems to render us impotent in the face of an indifferent cosmos and the inexorable pressure of Hobbesian social hostility. Yet, as I have suggested in the course of this work, the recognition of our mutual vulnerability and the acknowledgment and embrace of the otherness and mutuality that run "all the way down" in the structure of our freedom provide the locus for a "seeing good" amid and throughout the landscape of fracture that empowers transformative enactments of grace.

To that extent, an appropriate anthropology for a time of secularity will be one in which the questions "What is it to be human?" and "What does to mean to be human?" also encompass the concrete contextual question "What are we humans, situated in the finitude of vulnerability, freedom, and otherness, and

25 To be sure, such divisiveness is not peculiar to secular modernity; its pervasiveness, however, is especially challenging in view of the promise that, in its ideals of universal benevolence and impartial justice, modernity seemed to hold out for a steadily upward moral trajectory to peace among the peoples of the world.

dwelling in a world of multiplicity and broken meaning, called upon to be for one another and for our world?" My hope is that this work has provided a basis for framing one good answer to this question in the poignant images that Neiman, Taylor, Steiner, and Pope Francis provide for articulating the call of grace to be participant in the Triune enactment of the encompassing hospitality of God. In our finite and vulnerable humanity, we are called upon to enact a "seeing good" in and for the dynamics of fracture and division, a seeing good that empowers us "to pick up the pieces" of our fractured world by practices of inclusive hospitality and faithful accompaniment. In so doing we are enabled to become "guests to one another" in building a transformative culture of mercy and peace.

Bibliography

Works of Immanuel Kant

Kant, Immanuel. *Critique of the Power of Judgment* (cited as KU). *Kritik der Urteilskraft*, 1790 (AA 5:167–485). Cam: *Critique of the Power of Judgment: The Cambridge Edition of the Works of Immanuel Kant*, translated by Paul Guyer and Eric Matthews, 55–546. Cambridge: Cambridge University Press, 2000.*

———. *Critique of Practical Reason* (cited as CprR). *Kritik der praktischen Vernunft*, 1788 (AA 5:1–163). Cam: *Practical Philosophy: The Cambridge Edition of the Works of Immanuel Kant*, translated by Mary J. Gregor, 139–271. Cambridge: Cambridge University Press, 1999.

---

* The works of Kant quoted or referenced in the text are listed in the bibliography (along with their German titles) in alphabetical order according to their English translation titles. The English titles and translations of the works are from *The Cambridge Edition of the Works of Immanuel Kant*, Paul Guyer and Allen Wood, general editors (Cambridge: Cambridge University Press, 1993–2012). The bibliographical entry indicates the name of the translator and the title and page numbers of the volume in the Cambridge Edition (Cam) in which the translation appears. In the case of the *Critique of Pure Reason* page references use the standard convention A/B, in which A corresponds to the pagination of the 1st (1781) edition, and B corresponds to the pagination of the 2nd (1787) edition. Citations to the other works of Kant are referenced, first, to the pagination of the appropriate volume in the *Akademie Augabe* (AA), the critical edition of Kant's collected works (Immanuel Kant, *Kants Gesammelte Schriften* (Berlin: Königlich Preussischen Akademie der Wissenschaften, 1902), followed by the volume and page number, and then to the pagination of the translations in the Cambridge Edition (Cam)—e.g., KprV AA 5:146–48/Cam 257–58.

———. *Critique of Pure Reason* (cited as CPR). *Kritik der reinen Vernunft*, 1781; 2nd edition 1787 (AA 3–4). Cam: *Critique of Pure Reason*, translated by Paul Guyer and Eric Matthews. Cambridge: Cambridge University Press, 2000.

———. "First Introduction to the Critique of the Power of Judgment" (cited as EE). (1914). *Erste Einleitung in die Kritik der Urteilskraft* (AA 20:195–251). Cam: *Critique of the Power of Judgment: The Cambridge Edition of the Works of Immanuel Kant*, translated by Paul Guyer and Eric Matthews, 1–51. Cambridge: Cambridge University Press, 2000.

———. *Groundwork of the Metaphysics of Morals* (cited as G). *Grundlegung zur Metaphysik der Sitten*, 1785 (AA 4:385–463). Cam: *Practical Philosophy: The Cambridge Edition of the Works of Immanuel Kant*, translated by translated by Mary J. Gregor and Allen W. Wood, 43–108. Cambridge: Cambridge University Press, 1996.

———. *Jäsche Logic* (cited as JL). (1800) (AA 9:1–150). Cam: *Lectures on Logic: The Cambridge Edition of the Works of Immanuel Kant*, translated by J. Michael Young, 519–640. Cambridge: Cambridge University Press, 1992.

———. *Religion within the Boundaries of Mere Reason* (cited as R). *Die Religion innerhalb der Grenzen der blossen Vernunft*. 1793 (AA 6:1–202). Cam: *Religion within the Boundaries of Mere Reason: And Other Writings: Cambridge Texts in the History of Philosophy*, translated by George Di Giovanni and Allen Wood. Cambridge: Cambridge University Press, 1998.

Works Cited

Anderson Gold, Sharon. *Unnecessary Evil*. Albany: State University of New York Press, 2001.

Aquinas, Thomas. *Summa Theologiae*. Latin text and English translation, introductions, notes, appendices, and glossaries. Cambridge: New York: McGraw-Hill, 1964–1981.

Augustine. *Confessions*. Translated by F. J. Sheed. Introduction by Peter Brown. Indianapolis: Hackett, 2006.

Blackwood, Jeremy. "Lonergan and Rahner on the Natural Desire to See God." *Method*, n.s. 1, no. 2 (2010): 85–103.

Buckley, Michael. *At the Origins of Modern Atheism*. New Haven, CT: Yale University Press, 1987.

———. *Denying and Disclosing God: The Ambiguous Progress of Modern Atheism*. New Haven, CT: Yale University Press, 2004.

Burrell, David. *Knowing the Unknowable God: Ibn-Sina, Maimonides, Aquinas*. Notre Dame, IN: University of Notre Dame Press, 1986.

———. *Freedom and Creation in Three Traditions*. Notre Dame, IN: Notre Dame University Press, 1993.

———. "Creator/Creatures Relation: 'The Distinction' vs. 'Ontotheology'." *Faith and Philosophy* 25, no. 2 (2008): 177–89.

———. "Creation as Original Grace." In *God, Grace and Creation*, edited by Philip J. Rossi, 97–106. Maryknoll, NY: Orbis, 2010.

Coffey, David. "The Whole Rahner on the Supernatural Existential." *Theological Studies* 65, no. 1 (2004): 95–118.

Colorado, Carlos D. "Transcendent Sources and the Dispossession of the Self." In *Aspiring for Fullness in Secular Age: Essays on Religion and Theology in the Work of Charles Taylor*, edited by Carlos D. Colorado and Justin D. Classen, 82–92. Notre Dame IN: University of Notre Dame Press, 2014.

Donagan, Alan. *The Theory of Morality*. Chicago: University of Chicago Press, 1977.

Dorff, Elliot N. *The Way Into Tikkun Olam (Repairing the World)*. Woodstock, VT: Jewish Lights Publishing, 2005.

Dupré, Louis. *Passage to Modernity: An Essay in the Hermeneutics of Nature and Culture*. New Haven: Yale University Press, 1993.

Engstrom, Stephen. *The Form of Practical Knowledge: A Study of the Categorical Imperative*. Cambridge, MA: Harvard University Press, 2009.

Francis, Pope. "Fraternity, The Foundation and Pathway to Peace." Message for World Day of Peace. January 1, 2014.†

———. *Misericordia et Misera*. Apostolic Letter. November 20, 2016.

———. "Address to the Diplomatic Corps." January 9, 2017.

———. *Fratelli tutti*. Encyclical Letter on Fraternity and Social Friendship. October 3, 2020.

Frierson, Patrick. *Freedom and Anthropology in Kant's Moral Philosophy*. Cambridge: Cambridge University Press, 2003.

Goldmann, Lucien. *Immanuel Kant*. London: New Left Books [Verso], 1971. Translation of *La communauté humaine et l'univers chez Kant* (Paris: Presses Universitaires de France, 1948) and *Mensch, Gemeinschaft und Welt in der Philosophie Immanuel Kants* (Zurich: Europa Verlag, 1945).

Grenberg, Jeanine. *Kant and the Ethics of Humility: A Story of Dependence, Corruption and Virtue*. Cambridge: Cambridge University Press, 2005.

Halík, Tomáš. "Recognizing the Signs of the Times." In *Renewing the Church in a Secular Age: Holistic Dialogue and Kenotic Vision,* edited by Charles Taylor, José Casanova, George F. McLean, João J. Vila-Chã, 147–55. Cultural Heritage and Contemporary Change, Series VIII: Christian Philosophical Studies 21. Washington, DC: The Council for Research in Values and Philosophy, 2016.

Herdt, Jennifer A. "The Authentic Individual in the Network of Agape." In *Aspiring for Fullness in Secular Age: Essays on Religion and Theology in the Work of Charles Taylor*, edited by Carlos D. Colorado, 191–216. Notre Dame, IN: University of Notre Dame Press, 2014.

† Vatican documents available at www.vatican.va unless otherwise noted.

Hobson, Theo. "On Being a Perfect Guest: The Tablet Interview: George Steiner." *The Tablet* 259 (August 13, 2005): 15.

Jenson, Robert W. "Gratia non tollit naturam sed perficit." *Pro Ecclesia* 25, no. 1 (2016): 44–52.

Keenan, James F., SJ. "The World at Risk: Vulnerability, Precarity, and Connectedness," *Theological Studies* 81, no. 1 (2020): 132–49.

Kleingeld, Pauline. "Nature or Providence? On the Theoretical and Moral Importance of Kant's Philosophy of History." *American Catholic Philosophical Quarterly* 75, no. 2 (2001): 201–19.

Kuehn, Manfred. *Kant: A Biography*. Cambridge: Cambridge University Press, 2001.

Levinas, Emmanuel. "Useless Suffering." In *The Provocation of Levinas: Rethinking the Other*, edited by Robert Bernasconi and David Wood, 156–57. London: Routledge, 1988.

Louden, Robert. *Kant's Impure Ethics: From Rational Beings to Human Beings.* New York: Oxford University Press, 2000.

Munzel, G. Felicitas. *Kant's Conception of Moral Character*. Chicago: University of Chicago Press, 1999.

Myers, David N. "Herman Cohen and the Quest for Protestant Judaism." *Leo Baeck Institute Yearbook* 46, no. 1 (2001): 195–214.

Neiman, Susan. *The Unity of Reason: Rereading Kant*. New York: Oxford University Press, 1994.

———. *Evil in Modern Thought: An Alternative History of Philosophy*. Princeton: Princeton University Press, 2002.

———. *Moral Clarity: A Guide for Grown-Up Idealists*. Orlando: Harcourt, 2008.

Niebuhr, H. Richard. *The Responsible Self: An Essay in Christian Moral Philosophy*. New York: Harper & Row, 1963.

O'Connor, Flannery. "Revelation." In *Flannery O'Connor: Collected Works*, 633–54. New York: The Library of America, 1988.

Rawls, John. *A Theory of Justice*. Cambridge, MA: Belknap Press of Harvard University Press, 1971.

Rossi, Philip J., S.J. "War: The Social Form of Radical Evil." *Kant und die Berliner Aufklärung: Akten des IX. Internationalen Kant-Kongresses*, Band 4, edited by Volker Gerhardt, Rolf-Peter Horstmann and Ralph Schumacher, 248–56. Berlin, Walter de Gruyter, 2001.

———. "Divine Transcendence and the 'Languages of Personal Resonance': The Work of Charles Taylor as a Resource for Spirituality in an Era of Post-modernity." In *Theology and Conversation*, edited by J. Haers and P. DeMey, 783–94. Leuven: Peeters, 2004.

———. *The Social Authority of Reason*. Albany: State University of New York Press, 2005.

———. "Sojourners, Guests, and Strangers: The Church as Enactment of the Hospitality of God." *Questions liturgiques—Liturgical Questions* 90, nos. 2–3 (2009): 121–31.

———. "Seeing Good in a World of Suffering: Incarnation as God's Transforming Vision." In *Godhead Here in Hiding: Incarnation and the History of Human Suffering*, Bibliotheca Ephemeridum Theologicarum Lovaniensium 234, edited by Terrence Merrigan and Frederik Glorieux, 453–66. Leuven: Peeters, 2012.

———. "Cosmopolitanism: Kant's Social Anthropology of Hope." In *Kant und die Philosophie in weltbürgerlicher Absicht: Akten des XI. Kant-Kongresses 2010*, edited by Stefano Bacin, Alfredo Ferrarin, Claudio La Rocca, Margit Ruffing, Bd. 4:827–37. Berlin: Walter de Gruyter, 2013.

———. "The Crooked Wood of Human History: The Ethical Commonwealth and the Persistence of Evil." In *Nature and Freedom/Natur und Freiheit /Nature et Liberté; Proceedings of the XII. International Kant Congress*, edited by Violetta L. Waibel, Margit Ruffing, David Wagner, Bd. 4:2591–98. Berlin: Walter de Gruyter, 2018.

———. *The Ethical Commonwealth in History: Peace-Making as the Moral Vocation of Humanity*. Cambridge: Cambridge University Press, 2019.

———. "Human Freedom and the Triune God." In *T&T Clark Handbook of Theological Anthropology*, edited by Mary Ann Hinsdale and Stephen Oakey, 123–34. New York: Bloomsbury, 2021.

Sacks, Jonathan. *Not in God's Name: Confronting Religious Violence*. New York: Schocken Books, 2015.

Schweiker, William. "Human Flourishing and the Question of Fullness." In *Aspiring for Fullness in Secular Age: Essays on Religion and Theology in the Work of Charles Taylor*, edited by Carlos D. Colorado and Justin D. Classen, 127–51. Notre Dame, IN: University of Notre Dame Press, 2014.

Sokolowski, Robert. *The God of Faith and Reason*. Washington, DC: The Catholic University of America Press, 1995.

Steiner, George. *Real Presences*. Chicago: University of Chicago Press, 1989.

———. *Grammars of Creation*. New Haven, CT: Yale University Press, 2001.

Taylor, Charles. *Hegel*, Cambridge: Cambridge University Press, 1975.

———. "Introduction." *Human Agency and Language: Philosophical Papers I*, 1–12. Cambridge: Cambridge University Press, 1985.

———. "Self-Interpreting Animals." *Human Agency and Language: Philosophical Papers I*, 45–76. Cambridge: Cambridge University Press, 1985.

———. *Sources of the Self: The Making of the Modern Identity*. Cambridge, MA: Harvard University Press, 1989.

———. *Modern Social Imaginaries*. Durham, NC: Duke University Press, 2004.

———. *A Secular Age*. Cambridge, MA: Belknap Press of Harvard University Press, 2007.

———. "Buffered and Porous Selves." *The Immanent Frame* (Social Science Research Council blog), September 2, 2008. https://tif.ssrc.org/2008/09/02/buffered-and-porous-selves/.

———. *The Language Animal: The Full Shape of the Human Linguistic Capacity*. Cambridge, MA: Harvard University Press, 2016.

———. *Avenues of Faith: Conversations with Jonathan Guilbault*. Translated by Yvette Shalter. Waco, TX: Baylor University Press, 2020.

Vatican Council II. *Gaudium et Spes*. Pastoral Constitution on the Church in the Modern World. December 7, 1965.

Willey, Thomas E. *Back to Kant: The Revival of Kantianism in German Social and Historical Thought, 1860–1914*. Detroit: Wayne State University Press, 1978.

Wilson, Holly L. *Kant's Pragmatic Anthropology*. Albany: State University of New York Press, 2006.

Winter, Aloysius. *Der andere Kant: Zur philosophischen Theologie Immanuel Kants*. Hildesheim: Olms, 2000.

Index